15-Minute
ONE POT

Hollie Wood

EBURY
PRESS

15-Minute
ONE POT

Hollie Wood

EBURY
PRESS

8	Introduction	13	The Kitchen Bits I Couldn't Live Without
9	Pans I Use Throughout This Book	14	Easy Prep Guide
10	A Quick Note On Ingredients	15	Speedy Prep Tips
11	Freezing, Reheating And Keeping Leftovers	16	Your 5-minute Fixes

18 Speedy Classics

42 Fakeaways Fast

68 Comfort in a Flash

90 Pasta in a Pan

Rice & Easy	**114**
Wrap It Up	**140**
Cheesy & Indulgent	**166**
Sweet & Simple	**190**

Index	214
Conversion Tables	220
Acknowledgements	221
About The Author	222

Hi,

I'm Hollie, and I'm so glad you're here.

You might know me from social media, where I share easy, family-friendly dinners as @dinner_at_hols, but if not, hello! I'm Hollie, a mum of two, wife and full-time food lover from the Midlands.

I've always been surrounded by good food. I grew up in a proper foodie family, with a mum who always had something bubbling away on the hob. Home-cooked meals were a big part of my childhood – comforting, delicious and made with love.

When I became a mum myself, I knew I wanted to give that same feeling to my own kids, to raise them on dinners that were full of flavour, to help them enjoy trying new things, and to show them that cooking from scratch doesn't have to take hours.

My recipe-sharing journey started during lockdown, when my two were still very little. Life felt chaotic, and I started posting the dinners I was making, usually in a rush, often with the kids running around my feet. What began as a creative outlet quickly turned into a little community, and I realised I wasn't the only one trying to balance a love of food with real life.

And to now be writing this book, with Penguin, is honestly a dream come true. Having a book out with them is something I never thought would be possible. To hold it in my hands is something I can't quite put into words. I'm so proud of it, and so grateful that you're here with me.

Every recipe inside is made in one pot, ready in 15 minutes, and full of flavour. These are the kinds of dinners I cook for my own family every week, comforting, satisfying and realistic for busy evenings when you just need something quick, warm and crowd-pleasing.

Whether you're feeding your kids, your partner, your friends or just yourself, I hope these recipes bring you a little calm in the chaos. Less faff, less washing-up, and more time to actually enjoy your food (and your evening).

Here's to quick wins, cosy dinners and a little less stress at dinner time.

Hollie x

One pan.
Fifteen minutes.
Loads of flavour.

This book is packed with the kinds of dinners I cook at home all the time – quick, easy and made in one pan with no faff. These are meals that taste like you've made an effort, without actually having to. Whether you're rushing between school runs and after-work chaos, or you just want something delicious without loads of washing-up, this book's here to take the stress out of dinner time.

You'll find eight chapters full of inspiration, from Speedy Classics and Fakeaways Fast, to Cheesy and Indulgent and Sweet and Simple. Every single recipe is cooked in one pan and ready in around 15 minutes. I've tested them all again (and again) to make sure they work, taste amazing and fit into real life.

Pans I Use Throughout This Book

Every recipe in this book was made using just a few trusty, ovenproof pans, no gadgets or specialist kit required.

30cm, non-stick, oven-safe sauté pan with a lid

This is the one I use for most of the savoury dinners – it's big, roomy and deep enough to handle one-pan pastas, rice dishes and saucy bakes without bubbling over. An absolute workhorse.

20cm, non-stick, oven-safe frying pan

Used for some of the sweet puds in the Sweet and Simple chapter. Great for smaller desserts that start on the hob and finish in the oven.

26cm, non-stick, oven-safe frying pan

Perfect for smaller recipes or for anything that needs finishing in the oven, like loaded flatbreads or cheesy tops. If you've got one big oven-safe pan with a lid, plus a smaller one or two for bakes and puddings, you're good to go.

Standard baking tray

Only used once or twice, like for the pizza baguettes, but good to have around just in case.

A Quick Note On Ingredients

I've kept things as simple as possible, with ingredients you can easily pick up from UK supermarkets. Unless stated otherwise:

- All eggs are medium.
- Cheese is usually extra mature Cheddar or full-fat mozzarella, but use whatever you've got.
- Garlic purée, frozen onions and microwave rice are all totally allowed here – they save so much time (see my easy prep guide on page 14 for other handy hacks.
- Gnocchi is the fresh, chilled kind.
- Chicken is either breast or thigh depending on the recipe – both work, so feel free to swap if needed.
- Stock is made from cubes or pots, whichever you've got handy.
- I haven't noted gluten-free soy sauce in all recipes, so if you are gluten free, make sure you use gluten-free soy sauce or tamari.

Freezing, Reheating And Keeping Leftovers

Not every meal will freeze well, especially some of the creamy ones, but I've marked the ones that are freezer-friendly with a ❄ so you know which you can batch-cook or stash for later.

When reheating, always make sure food is first fully defrosted and then heated until piping hot throughout. Some gnocchi and pasta dishes are best eaten fresh but will keep for 3 or 4 days in the fridge, then reheat fine with a splash of stock or water to loosen the sauce.

The recipe key

Look out for these little icons next to recipes:

V — Veggie – suitable for vegetarians.

GF — Gluten-free – naturally gluten-free or easily adapted (just make sure you choose gluten-free options, where needed).

❄ — Freezer-friendly – great to batch-cook and freeze.

The Kitchen Bits I Couldn't Live Without

I'm not big on fancy gadgets or anything that takes longer to clean than it does to use, but there are a few things I reach for every single day that just make one-pot cooking quicker, easier and way less faffy. These aren't expensive or complicated, just proper helpful. If you're setting up your own quick-dinner kit, here's where I'd start:

MY RIDE-OR-DIE FRYING PAN
Big enough to hold a full family meal, deep enough to take sauces and pasta, and non-stick so nothing catches (and washing-up is a dream). I use mine for nearly every recipe in this book. I'd always go for one that's oven-safe, too – it gives you more flexibility when finishing off bakes or melts. If you invest in one thing, make it this.

SILICONE SPATULA OR SPOONULA
(the bendy kind)
I've got a couple of these and I use them for everything – stirring, scraping down sides, folding sauces. They don't scratch your pan and they're way better than wooden spoons for scooping up every last bit.

KITCHEN SCISSORS
Not the most glamorous, but honestly a game-changer. I use them to snip bacon straight into the pan, slice spring onions, even cut herbs when I can't be bothered to get the chopping board out.

GARLIC PRESS OR GARLIC PURÉE
I love garlic in pretty much everything, and using a garlic press just makes it so much quicker. No peeling or faffing. Garlic purée is also a staple in my fridge and makes life easier when time's tight.

A PROPER SET OF MEASURING SPOONS
Because guessing a tablespoon with a dessertspoon never ends well. I've got a magnetic set that sticks together so they don't disappear into the drawer abyss.

MINI GRATER/ZESTER
Perfect for Parmesan, lemon zest or even grating garlic straight into the pan when you're in a rush. Small but mighty.

MINI JUG FOR LIQUIDS
So handy for measuring out stock, milk, cream, anything you need in a quick pour. I use mine to heat liquids in the microwave too and it saves faffing about with extra pans.

KITCHEN TIMER
(or let's be honest, your phone or Alexa)
Because getting distracted while cooking is basically my default setting. I set timers constantly: one for the pan, one for the oven, one for reminding me to sit down and drink a cuppa.

This isn't about having a cupboard full of kit, it's about knowing what helps you get dinner done without the stress. These tools make one-pot cooking feel a little less like a chore and a bit more like your superpower.

Easy Prep Guide

Let's be honest, we all love a home-cooked dinner… but not the endless peeling, chopping, and faffing that can come with it. These are my go-to cheats to get dinner on the table faster, because no one needs to be crying over an onion on a Wednesday night.

FROZEN CHOPPED ONIONS
Straight from freezer to pan. No tears, no waste, no 'Oh, this one's gone a bit soft in the cupboard' moments.

GARLIC AND GINGER PURÉES
No peeling, no grating, no sticky fingers. Just squeeze or spoon straight into the pan for instant flavour.

MICROWAVE RICE
Cuts 15 minutes off cooking time and still tastes great. Ideal for one-pot meals and stir-fries.

PRE-GRATED CHEESE
Perfect for when you don't fancy wrestling with the grater (and eating half the block in the process).

FROZEN VEG
Spinach, broccoli, peppers, peas, carrots, prepped, washed, and ready to chuck in.

JARRED PESTOS, PASTES AND SAUCES
A quick spoonful can add depth and richness without having to make your own from scratch.

COOKED CHICKEN OR RÔTISSERIE CHICKEN
Great for throwing into wraps, pasta or salads when you really can't face turning the oven on.

TINNED POTATOES
Slice them, season them, fry them – crispy golden potatoes in minutes.

PRE-WASHED SALAD BAGS
Tip straight onto the plate and pretend you've been lovingly tearing leaves all afternoon.

TINNED BEANS AND LENTILS
No soaking, no boiling – just drain and add for instant protein.

FRESH PASTA
Cooks in just a few minutes, so you can get dinner on the table even faster. Perfect for creamy sauces or quick pasta bakes.

Remember, shortcuts aren't 'cheating'. They're the difference between getting dinner done or giving up and ordering a takeaway. And honestly? No one's checking if you peeled that onion yourself.

Speedy Prep Tips

Getting dinner on the table in 15 minutes is easier when you've got a few tricks up your sleeve. These are the habits I use in my own kitchen to save time and keep things stress-free.

READ THE RECIPE FIRST
Sounds obvious, but knowing what's coming next means you can prep in the right order and avoid last-minute scrambles.

GROUP INGREDIENTS BY USE
Keep everything for each stage of the recipe together so you're not hunting around mid-cook.

USE A BIG CHOPPING BOARD
More room = less clutter, and you can chop everything in one go without stopping to clear space.

PREP WHILE YOU COOK
If onions are softening in the pan, chop your peppers or measure your spices at the same time.

GET YOUR PANS AND UTENSILS OUT FIRST
Saves you from rummaging through cupboards with messy hands.

SHARPEN YOUR KNIVES
A sharp knife makes chopping quicker, easier and safer.

KEEP WASTE BOWLS ON THE COUNTER
Toss peels and scraps into a small bowl so you're not running to the bin mid-prep.

BATCH-CHOP
If you use onions, peppers and garlic often, chop extra and store them in the fridge or freezer for later in the week.

MEASURE STRAIGHT INTO THE PAN
Skip extra bowls where you can – fewer dishes to wash means a quicker clean-up.

Your 5-minute Fixes

We've all been there – you're halfway through cooking, something's gone a bit wrong, and you're wondering if you should just give up and order a takeaway. Don't panic. I've got you. Here's how to save dinner in five minutes or less.

SAUCE TOO THICK?
Add a splash of stock, pasta cooking water or milk and stir until you reach the right consistency.

SAUCE TOO THIN?
Simmer uncovered for a couple of minutes, or stir in a spoonful of cream cheese or a slurry of cornflour and water.

TOO SALTY?
Balance it with a squeeze of lemon juice, a spoonful of cream cheese or a splash of milk.

TOO SPICY?
Stir in extra cream cheese, yoghurt or coconut milk. Serving with bread or rice on the side will also help cool it down.

TOO BLAND?
Add extra seasoning, a squeeze of lemon or lime, a dash of hot sauce or some fresh herbs.

PASTA NOT COOKED THROUGH?
Add a splash more stock, cover with a lid and simmer for another minute or two.

CHEESE NOT MELTING?
Lower the heat slightly, cover the pan and give it a minute – the steam will do the job.

DINNER READY TOO EARLY?
Pop a lid on the pan and keep the heat on low – it'll stay warm without overcooking.

Speedy Classics

Veg-packed Spaghetti Bolognese

❄ SAUCE ONLY   **SERVES 4**   **CALORIES: 497**

Spray oil
500g lean 5% beef mince
1 onion, grated
1 medium carrot, grated
1 courgette, grated
2 peppers, finely diced
3 tsp garlic purée or 3 garlic cloves, chopped
1 tbsp tomato purée
1 tbsp dried mixed herbs
1 beef stockpot/cube
500g passata
400ml boiling water
500g fresh pasta (I use penne, but any pasta shape will work fine)
80g Parmesan, grated
A handful of fresh parsley, chopped, to garnish

Speedy Bolognese is one of those dinners that just works for our family. It's the kind of meal I know my kids will devour without a fuss, and it always brings that bit of comfort we all need after a busy day. Simple, satisfying and a firm favourite in our house.

1. Spray a large pan with oil and place over a medium to high heat. Add the beef mince and cook until it's browned, then add all the veg, garlic, tomato purée, mixed herbs and stockpot/cube.
2. Cook for a couple of minutes, then add the passata, water and fresh pasta.
3. Cook over a medium heat for 5–6 minutes, or until the pasta is cooked through, then sprinkle with Parmesan and chopped parsley and serve.

SWAPS

→ Swap beef mince for turkey or chicken mince. A leaner option that still gives a rich, meaty flavour.
→ Swap regular pasta for wholewheat or red lentil pasta. Boosts fibre and adds extra plant-based protein.
→ Add extra veg like courgette, spinach or mushrooms. Helps bulk it out and sneaks in more nutrients for the kids.

SIDES

+ **Garlicky wilted spinach.** Super quick, super tasty, just throw it in a pan with a bit of garlic for a couple of minutes.
+ **A crisp side salad.** Something fresh to cut through the richness – rocket, cucumber, whatever's in the fridge.
+ **Buttery garlic bread.** Golden, crunchy and perfect for scooping up every last bit of that bolognese.

Hunter's Chicken Sausages and Mediterranean Veggies

 GF **SERVES 4** **CALORIES: 439**

Spray oil
10 gluten-free chicken chipolata sausages, approx. 400g
10 rashers of streaky bacon
1 red onion, thinly sliced
4 peppers (mixed colours), thinly sliced
1 courgette, sliced
Salt and black pepper, to taste
3 tsp garlic purée or 3 garlic cloves, chopped
1 tbsp smoked paprika
½ tbsp dried oregano
1 tbsp tomato purée
100ml hot chicken stock
4 tbsp BBQ sauce
60g extra mature Cheddar, grated
60g full-fat mozzarella, grated
Chopped fresh parsley, to garnish (optional)

This one feels like a bit of a cheat, but in the best way. All the flavours of hunter's chicken, but made quicker, lighter and with sausages (which my lot always prefer anyway!). The roasted Mediterranean veggies add a pop of colour and goodness, and it all just works. It's one of those throw-it-together meals that feels a bit special, even when the day's been anything but.

1. Spray a large frying pan with oil and place over a medium to high heat. Wrap each sausage in a rasher of bacon and put them straight into the pan. Cook for around 6–7 minutes, turning often, until they're browned and starting to crisp up.

2. Add the red onion, peppers and courgette. Season with salt and black pepper, then stir in the garlic purée, paprika, oregano and tomato purée. Pour in the hot chicken stock, give everything a good stir, and pop a lid on the pan.

3. Let it all cook for 5–6 minutes, until the sausages are cooked through and the veg have softened. Spoon the BBQ sauce over the sausages and scatter over both cheeses. Pop the lid back on for 1–2 minutes, until the cheese is melted and gooey – or you can pop it under the grill. Finish with chopped parsley if you fancy, and serve it all up straight from the pan. So much flavour, barely any washing up!

SWAPS

→ Swap chicken sausages for pork, beef or veggie sausages. Use whatever you fancy, they all work a treat.
→ Swap the veg for mushrooms, aubergine, spinach or frozen peas/sweetcorn. A great way to use up whatever's in the fridge or freezer.
→ Swap the cheese for Red Leicester, Gouda or cream cheese. Perfect if you're running low on Cheddar or you fancy something a bit different.

SIDES

+ **Spoon over rice or couscous.** Perfect for soaking up all that saucy goodness.
+ **Serve with crispy potatoes or mash.** Great for a cosy, comfort food vibe.
+ **Stuff into a warm baguette.** Messy, delicious and totally worth it.

Smoky Chicken Fajitas

SERVES 4 **CALORIES: 509 (PER 2 MINI WRAPS)**

Spray oil
500g chicken breast, thinly sliced
Salt and black pepper, to taste
1 red onion, thinly sliced
3 peppers (mixed colours), thinly sliced
3 tsp garlic purée or 3 garlic cloves, chopped
1 tbsp smoked paprika
1 tsp ground cumin
1 tsp dried oregano
1 tbsp tomato purée
Juice of ½ a lime
120g cheese, grated (I use extra mature Cheddar)

TO SERVE
Chopped fresh coriander or parsley (optional)
8 mini wraps
Your favourite toppings (we used sour cream, salsa and guac)

We have made fajitas more times than I can count! They are one of those dinners that no one complains about (a small miracle!). This version is super speedy and full of smoky flavour. We love piling it into warm wraps with whatever toppings we've got in the fridge. No fuss, no complaints and barely any washing-up – what more could you want?!

1. Spray a large frying pan with oil and place over a medium to high heat. Add the sliced chicken, season with salt and black pepper and cook for 5–6 minutes, until golden and nearly cooked through.
2. Add the sliced onion and peppers along with the garlic purée, paprika, cumin, oregano and tomato purée. Stir it all together so the chicken and veg are coated in the spices.
3. Squeeze over the lime juice, then pop a lid on the pan and cook for another 5–6 minutes, stirring halfway, until the veg are soft and starting to char and the chicken is cooked through.
4. Sprinkle over the cheese and put the lid on so it melts slightly. Garnish with chopped coriander or parsley, if you like, and serve it all up straight from the pan with the warm wraps and all your favourite toppings.

SWAPS

→ Swap chicken for prawns or thinly sliced beef, or even for tofu or halloumi for a veggie version. Great if you fancy a change or want to use up what's in the fridge.

→ Use fajita seasoning or taco mix instead of individual spices. A quick shortcut when you're in a rush.

SIDES

+ **Crispy oven chips.** Quick, easy and perfect for scooping up all the extra filling.
+ **Zesty corn salad.** Sweetcorn, lime, red onion and a pinch of chilli – fresh, crunchy and takes no time at all to make.
+ **Spiced rice.** Cook up a quick batch with cumin, paprika and a squeeze of lime – perfect on the side or piled into your wrap.

Cheat's Lasagne

❄ SAUCE ONLY   **SERVES 4**   **CALORIES: 415**

Spray oil
1 onion, grated
1 carrot, grated
3 tsp garlic purée
500g lean 5% beef mince
1 tbsp tomato purée
1 tsp dried oregano
500ml passata
1 beef stock cube
Salt and black pepper, to taste
200g fresh lasagne sheets, cut into wide strips
80g cheese, grated (I use extra mature Cheddar)
Chopped fresh parsley, to garnish (optional)

FOR THE WHITE SAUCE
100g cream cheese
1 tsp Dijon mustard
100ml semi-skimmed milk (adjust to loosen)
½ tsp garlic granules

Lasagne is one of those dinners that feels like a warm hug, and it just so happens to be my son Harry's absolute favourite. But much as I'd love to make the full layered version every time he asks, I don't always have hours to spend in the kitchen. This cheat's version gives you all the comfort and flavour of the classic, but it's ready in just 15 minutes. It's hearty, creamy and so satisfying, with no faff and barely any washing-up.

1. Spray a large, deep frying pan with oil and place over a medium to high heat. Add the grated onion and carrot and cook for 2–3 minutes, until starting to soften.
2. Add the garlic purée and beef mince, and cook until the mince is browned, breaking it up with a spoon as it cooks. Stir in the tomato purée and oregano, then pour in the passata and crumble in the beef stock cube. Season with salt and black pepper, if needed, and let it simmer for 5–6 minutes, until slightly thickened.
3. While the Bolognese simmers, whisk or blend together the cream cheese, mustard, milk, garlic granules and a pinch of salt and black pepper until smooth.
4. Stir the fresh lasagne strips into the Bolognese. Let the pasta cook for 4–5 minutes until tender, adding a splash of milk or water if the sauce thickens too much.
5. Pour the creamy white sauce over the top and gently swirl it through the Bolognese. Scatter over the grated cheese, then pop a lid on and let the cheese melt into the sauce. Serve hot, straight from the pan, with a sprinkle of chopped parsley, if you like.

SWAPS

→ **Swap beef mince for turkey, chicken mince or even tinned lentils and the beef cube for a veg one.** A leaner version that still brings loads of flavour.
→ **Swap lasagne sheets for a different shape of fresh pasta.** Same comforting vibe.

SIDES

+ **A crisp green salad.** Fresh rocket or mixed leaves with a balsamic drizzle, perfect for balancing the richness.
+ **Garlic bread or crusty rolls.** Because lasagne and garlic bread just belong together.
+ **Steamed greens.** Tenderstem broccoli or green beans, quick to cook and they add a bit of crunch and colour to the plate.

Meatball Marinara Subs with a Crunchy Slaw

SERVES 4 **CALORIES: 536**

These subs are always a bit of a free-for-all in our house – sauce flying, kids hovering with their rolls ready, and someone usually ends up with cheese in their hair. But honestly, that's what makes them so loved. They've got that fakeaway feel, but they're speedy, satisfying and guaranteed to keep everyone quiet (for five minutes, at least).

FOR THE MEATBALL SUBS
- Spray oil
- Approx. 20 mini meatballs (around 350g)
- 1 small onion, finely diced
- 2 tsp garlic purée or 2 garlic cloves, chopped
- 1 tbsp tomato purée
- 1 tsp dried oregano
- 500g passata
- 1 chicken stockpot/cube
- Salt and black pepper, to taste
- 80g full-fat mozzarella or extra mature Cheddar, grated
- 4 soft sub rolls

FOR THE CRUNCHY SLAW
- ½ a small red cabbage, finely shredded
- 1 carrot, grated
- 2 tbsp 0% Greek yoghurt
- 2 tbsp light mayo
- 1 tsp Dijon mustard or a splash of vinegar

1. Spray a large frying pan with oil and place over a medium to high heat. Add the meatballs and brown them all over, about 5 minutes. Add the chopped onion and cook for 2–3 minutes, until soft, then stir in the garlic, tomato purée and oregano. Pour in the passata, then add the stockpot/cube, season to taste and mix well.
2. While that's bubbling away, mix together all the slaw ingredients in a bowl, season to taste, and pop it into the fridge until you're ready to serve.
3. Once the sauce is thick and the meatballs are cooked through, scatter the cheese over the top, then pop a lid on the pan and let it melt for 1–2 minutes.
4. Split your sub rolls, add the crunchy slaw and pile in the cheesy meatballs and sauce. Get your napkins ready, as these are gloriously messy!

SWAPS

- → Swap meatballs for chicken, turkey or sausage meatballs. Still juicy and packed with flavour, great for a speedy homemade version.
- → Swap sub rolls for brioche buns, baguettes or soft pittas. Works just as well, alternatively you can turn it into a cosy bowl with pasta or rice.

SIDES

- + **Crispy potato wedges.** Straight from the oven or air fryer, golden, fluffy and made for dunking in any leftover sauce.
- + **Pickled pink onions.** Sharp, tangy and the perfect little pop of flavour against the rich marinara.
- + **Garlic butter corn on the cob.** Quick to make and totally worth it, buttery, garlicky and so good with the crunchy slaw.

Beef and Butterbean Stroganoff

GF · **SERVES 4** · **CALORIES: 275**

Spray oil
1 onion, finely chopped
2 garlic cloves, crushed
500g lean 5% beef mince
1 tsp smoked paprika
1 tsp dried thyme
1 tbsp tomato purée
200ml hot beef stock
1 tbsp Worcestershire sauce
1 x 400g tin of butterbeans, drained and rinsed
150g 0% Greek yoghurt or crème fraîche
Salt and black pepper, to taste
Fresh parsley, chopped, to finish

This is a real family favourite, hearty, comforting, and packed full of protein to keep us all full after a busy day. Using lean beef mince and creamy butterbeans, it's a simple way to get a nourishing meal on the table that everyone enjoys. It's one of those recipes I turn to when I want something satisfying but without any fuss, perfect for those moments when you just want good, honest food that hits the spot.

1. Spray a large frying pan with oil and place over a medium to high heat. Add the onion and cook for 2 minutes, until softened. Add the garlic and beef mince, breaking the meat up as it browns.
2. Stir in the paprika, thyme and tomato purée, and cook for 1 minute. Pour in the hot beef stock and Worcestershire sauce, then add the butterbeans. Bring to a simmer and cook for 7–8 minutes, stirring occasionally, until the sauce thickens slightly and the beans are heated through.
3. Remove from the heat and stir in the Greek yoghurt or crème fraîche until creamy. Season with salt and black pepper. Serve straight from the pan, sprinkled with fresh parsley.

SWAPS

→ **Swap beef mince for turkey mince.** A leaner alternative that still gives loads of flavour.
→ **Swap butterbeans for cannellini beans.** A creamy bean that keeps the texture soft but with a slightly milder taste.
→ **Swap Greek yoghurt for cream cheese.** Adds a rich, creamy finish and melts right into the sauce.

SIDES

+ **Crusty bread.** Perfect for mopping up all that creamy stroganoff sauce – warm crusty bread makes it extra comforting and satisfying.
+ **Rice.** For a super quick and easy meal, serve your stroganoff straight over hot microwave rice. Ready in minutes and fuss-free!
+ **Roasted or steamed veggies.** Serve alongside your favourite roasted or steamed vegetables, such as broccoli, green beans or carrots, for a lighter, veggie-packed option.

Chicken Chow Mein

SERVES 4 **CALORIES: 380**

Spray oil
500g chicken breasts, thinly sliced
1 onion, thinly sliced
3 tsp garlic purée
3 tsp ginger purée
2 red peppers, thinly sliced
150g broccoli florets
2 x 150g straight-to-wok egg noodles
3 tbsp soy sauce
1 tbsp oyster sauce
1 tsp sesame oil (optional)

TO FINISH
Spring onions, chopped
Sesame seeds (optional)

I've made this chow mein more times than I can count, and it's one of those meals that never lets me down. When the day's been full-on and I just want something easy but properly tasty, this is what I reach for. It's packed with flavour, a great way to use up whatever veg I've got knocking about, and the kids always clear their plates (which is a win in itself!). It's got that lovely fakeaway feel, but with all the ease of a weeknight throw-together.

1. Spray a large frying pan or wok with oil and place over a medium to high heat. Add the chicken and cook for 5–6 minutes, until browned and cooked through.
2. Add the onion, garlic purée and ginger purée to the pan and cook for 2 minutes, until fragrant.
3. Toss in the red peppers and broccoli florets and stir-fry for 4–5 minutes, until just tender.
4. Add the egg noodles, soy sauce, oyster sauce and sesame oil. Toss everything together and cook for a final 2 minutes, until everything's heated through and coated in the sauce.
5. Finish with chopped spring onions and with sesame seeds, if you fancy.

SWAPS

→ **Swap chicken for prawns.** Use 400g of raw king prawns for a lighter seafood version – they cook in minutes!

→ **Make it veggie with mixed beans.** A drained tin works perfectly and adds plenty of plant-based protein.

→ **Swap egg noodles for udon.** Thick, chewy and ready to throw straight into the pan, no extra prep needed.

SIDES

+ **Steamed dumplings.** A few gyoza or dim sum-style dumplings on the side turn it into a proper street-food-style feast.
+ **Fried egg on top.** Soft yolk, golden edges, adds richness and takes it up a level.
+ **Pickled veggies.** Quick pickled cucumber or radish brings a fresh, zingy contrast to all that savoury goodness.

Speedy Classics

Chicken, Bacon and Tarragon Pot Pie

SERVES 4 **CALORIES: 627**

2 tbsp unsalted butter (I use light)
150g diced smoked bacon (I use lean)
2 tbsp plain flour
400ml hot chicken stock
100g light cream cheese
1 heaped tsp Dijon mustard (optional)
1½ tsp dried tarragon (or 1½ tbsp fresh tarragon, chopped)
400g cooked chicken, shredded (rôtisserie or leftovers)
Salt and black pepper, to taste
A large handful of frozen peas or baby spinach (optional)
1 sheet of ready-rolled puff pastry
1 egg, beaten

This is my go-to on a lazy Sunday when I want all the comfort of a proper home-cooked meal, but I can't be bothered with loads of prep or a sink full of washing-up. It's creamy, cosy, and feels like the kind of thing you'd eat with your feet up and a glass of wine in hand. The puff pastry turns golden and crisp under the grill, and the filling is full of flavour but super simple – just chuck it all into one pan and let it do its thing. It's everything I love about a Sunday dinner, minus the stress.

1. Start by heating the butter in a large ovenproof frying pan over a medium to high heat. Add the diced bacon and cook for a couple of minutes, until just starting to turn golden.
2. Stir in the plain flour and let it cook for about a minute, stirring constantly to form a paste. Gradually pour in the hot chicken stock, whisking as you go, until the sauce is smooth and starting to bubble.
3. Stir in the cream cheese, Dijon mustard (if using), and tarragon, and keep stirring until the cream cheese melts into the sauce and it's looking lovely and creamy. Add the shredded cooked chicken, season with salt and black pepper, and throw in a handful of frozen peas or spinach if you fancy.
4. Let everything bubble together for a minute so the flavours can mingle, then take the pan off the heat. Cut the sheet of pastry into 4–5cm squares, and pop them on top of the filling in the pan.
5. Brush the pastry with beaten egg, then pop the whole pan under a hot oven grill (around 220°C/200°C fan) for 5–7 minutes, or until the pastry is puffed up and golden. Spoon it out straight from the pan and enjoy that creamy, herby goodness with the flaky golden pastry on top. Proper comfort food, and barely any washing-up.

SWAPS

→ **Swap tarragon for thyme or parsley.** Still herby and fragrant, but you can leave it out altogether if you've got picky eaters at the table.

→ **Swap cream cheese for crème fraîche or double cream.** Both add a lovely richness, and garlic and herb cream cheese works too, for a little extra flavour.

→ **Swap puff pastry for cheesy croutons or garlic bread slices.** You still get that golden, crispy finish without the faff of pastry.

SIDES

+ **Garlicky wilted spinach.** Super quick, super tasty, just throw it into a pan for a couple of minutes.
+ **A crisp side salad.** Something fresh to cut through the richness – rocket, cucumber, whatever's in the fridge.
+ **Creamy mashed potatoes.** Because sometimes you just want full-on comfort. No judgement here.

Coronation Chicken and Potatoes

GF **SERVES 4** **CALORIES: 446**

Spray oil
500g chicken breast, diced
1 tbsp curry powder
1 tsp garlic granules
1 tsp onion granules
1 small red onion, finely diced
1 x 400g tin of new potatoes, drained and halved
75g light mayo
100g light cream cheese
30g sultanas or raisins
1 tbsp mango chutney
Salt and black pepper, to taste
Chopped fresh coriander or parsley, to serve (optional)

I grabbed a tin of potatoes the other day and honestly, I'll never look back. This Coronation chicken and potato mash-up is my lazy girl dinner hack – minimal effort, maximum flavour. It's sweet, tangy, a little bit spicy, and the sultanas give it that proper retro throwback. No peeling, no faff... just dinner on the table before the kids ask for snacks again.

1. Spray a large pan with oil and place over a medium to high heat. Add the chicken, curry powder, garlic granules and onion granules and fry for 5–6 minutes, until golden and cooked through.
2. Add the red onion and tinned potatoes and cook for another 2–3 minutes, stirring often.
3. Turn the heat down low and stir in the mayo, cream cheese, sultanas/raisins and mango chutney. Mix until everything is creamy and coated in the sauce.
4. Season with salt and black pepper, sprinkle over some chopped herbs, if you like, and serve.

SWAPS

→ **Swap chicken breast for rôtisserie chicken.** Great for using up leftovers and cuts down cooking time.
→ **Swap tinned potatoes for cooked new potatoes.** Perfect if you've got leftovers in the fridge.
→ **Swap mango chutney for apricot jam.** Still gives a sweet tangy finish if you're out of chutney.

SIDES

+ **Warm naan or pitta.** Great for scooping up all that creamy sauce.
+ **Minted cucumber salad.** Adds freshness and crunch.
+ **Quick pickled onions.** Cuts through the creaminess with a tangy bite.

Veg and Halloumi Shakshuka

SERVES 4 **CALORIES: 350**

Spray oil
1 large onion, finely sliced
2 red peppers, thinly sliced
2 courgettes, halved lengthways and sliced
1½ tsp garlic purée
1½ tsp smoked paprika
1 tsp ground cumin
1½ tsp dried oregano
250g reduced-fat halloumi, sliced
1 x 400g tin of chopped tomatoes
250ml passata
Salt and black pepper, to taste
4 eggs
Fresh parsley or coriander, to finish (optional)

This shakshuka is one of those meals my kids actually get excited about, which is basically a win in my book! It's colourful, easy and somehow feels a bit special without me having to faff about. Perfect for those evenings when I want to get dinner on the table quickly but still keep everyone happy.

1. Spray a large frying pan with oil and place over a medium heat. Add the onion, peppers and courgettes and cook for around 4 minutes, until they're starting to soften.
2. Stir in the garlic purée, paprika, cumin and oregano and cook for another minute, until fragrant. Move the veg to one side of the pan and lay the halloumi slices on the other.
3. Cook the halloumi for 1–2 minutes on each side, until golden, then stir it into the veg. Pour in the chopped tomatoes and passata, season with salt and black pepper, and let it bubble for 2–3 minutes to thicken slightly.
4. Create 4 wells in the sauce and crack an egg into each one. Cover the pan with a lid or foil and cook for 5–6 minutes, or until the egg whites are set and the yolks are still a little runny. Finish with a scattering of herbs, if you like.

SWAPS

→ **Swap halloumi for chicken strips.** Adds extra protein and gives the dish a meatier bite.
→ **Swap red pepper for roasted aubergine.** Smoky, soft and goes perfectly with that rich tomato sauce.
→ **Swap courgettes for fresh spinach.** Wilts down beautifully and adds a leafy green boost with no extra fuss.

SIDES

+ **Crusty bread.** Perfect for dipping into the rich sauce and runny egg yolks.
+ **Buttery mashed potatoes.** Creamy mashed potatoes soak up the saucy shakshuka perfectly, for a comforting meal.
+ **Simple green salad.** A fresh side of mixed leaves with lemon juice and olive oil cuts through the richness and adds crunch.

Lamb Tikka Masala

❄ GF SERVES 4 CALORIES: 266

Spray oil
500g lean diced lamb
1 onion, finely diced
1 tbsp garlic purée
1 tbsp ginger purée
1 tbsp tikka curry paste
2 tbsp tomato purée
1 tsp ground cumin
1 tsp ground coriander
½ tsp paprika
500g passata
100ml single cream
Salt and black pepper, to taste
Chopped fresh coriander, to finish (optional)

This one's a proper fakeaway favourite in our house. Rich, creamy lamb tikka that tastes like a treat but takes no time at all. It's the kind of dinner that makes you feel like you've got your life together, even if the rest of the day has been chaos.

1. Spray a large pan with oil and place over a medium to high heat. Add the lamb and cook for 3–4 minutes, until browned all over, then push it to one side of the pan.
2. Add the diced onion to the other side and cook for another couple of minutes, until starting to soften.
3. Stir in the garlic purée and ginger purée, tikka curry paste, tomato purée and ground spices.
4. Cook for 30 seconds, then mix everything together and pour in the passata. Give it a good stir and let it bubble away for 5–6 minutes, until the lamb is cooked through and the sauce has thickened slightly. Lower the heat and stir in the cream.
5. Let it gently warm through for another minute, then taste and season if needed.
6. Finish with a sprinkling of chopped coriander, if you fancy, and serve straight from the pan.

SWAPS

→ **Swap lamb for chicken breast.** A leaner and quicker-cooking option that still soaks up all the flavour.
→ **Swap single cream for 0% Greek yoghurt.** Lower in fat and adds a nice tang – just stir it in off the heat to prevent it splitting.
→ **Swap tikka paste for mild curry powder.** Great if you don't have paste on hand – use 1½ tsp and add a splash of lemon juice to brighten the flavour.

SIDES

+ **Ready-to-eat naan breads.** Warm them briefly in the microwave or toaster for a soft, pillowy side.
+ **Microwave basmati or pilau rice.** Quick, no-fuss and done in 2 minutes, ideal for weeknights.
+ **Crispy poppadoms.** Store-bought versions are perfect for scooping and dipping, no prep needed.

Fish Pie Gnocchi

❄ **SERVES 4**   **CALORIES: 492**

This one ticks all the boxes: creamy, comforting, packed with flavour, and you don't even have to peel a single potato. Think cosy fish pie meets gnocchi bake, all bubbling away in one pan. Perfect for when you fancy something hearty but still want dinner on the table fast.

Spray oil
1 small onion, finely diced
Salt and black pepper, to taste
2 tsp garlic purée
1 tbsp plain flour
400ml semi-skimmed milk
1 pack of fish pie mix (approx. 320g – salmon, smoked haddock and white fish)
500g gnocchi
1 tsp Dijon mustard
100g frozen peas
150g cooked prawns
40g extra mature Cheddar, grated
Chopped fresh chives, to serve (optional)

1. Spray a large pan with oil and place over a medium heat. Add the onion, season with a little salt and cook for 3–4 minutes, until starting to soften.
2. Stir in the garlic purée and cook for another 30 seconds, then sprinkle over the flour and stir to coat everything. Gradually add the milk, stirring continuously to avoid lumps, until it forms a smooth sauce.
3. Add the fish pie mix and gnocchi, then simmer for 4–5 minutes, until the fish is just cooked through and the gnocchi are soft.
4. Stir in the mustard, peas, prawns and Cheddar. Let it bubble for 1–2 minutes to melt the cheese and warm everything through.
5. Season to taste with salt and black pepper, garnish with chopped chives, if using, and serve hot.

SWAPS

→ **Swap milk for fish or vegetable stock.** A lighter base that still adds flavour if you're avoiding dairy.
→ **Swap prawns for cooked chicken or turkey.** A non-seafood alternative that still keeps it high in protein.
→ **Swap gnocchi for cooked pasta.** Great if you've got pasta in the cupboard but no gnocchi on hand.

SIDES

+ **Steamed green beans.** Adds freshness and crunch to balance the creamy sauce.
+ **Lemon-dressed rocket salad.** Cuts through the richness with a bit of zing.
+ **Crusty wholemeal bread.** Perfect for mopping up that fish-pie-style sauce.

Fakeaways Fast

Salt and Pepper Chicken Stir-fry

 GF **SERVES 4** **CALORIES: 320**

Spray oil
500g chicken breast, thinly sliced
1 tsp cornflour (optional, for extra crispiness)
1 tsp sea salt, or to taste
1 tsp freshly ground black pepper
1 tsp Chinese five-spice
1 tsp chilli flakes (adjust to taste)
1 small red onion, thinly sliced
1 red pepper, sliced
1 yellow pepper, sliced
1 tbsp garlic purée
1 fresh red chilli, thinly sliced (optional, for extra kick)

TO FINISH
2 spring onions, chopped
Chopped fresh coriander (optional)

Whenever life's busy and I'm juggling a million things, this salt and pepper stir-fry saves the day. It's packed with flavour, super easy and even the kids ask for more, always a win in my book! Plus, when it's all done in one pan, it means less washing-up. Sorted.

1. Spray a large frying pan or wok with oil and put on a medium-high heat. Toss the sliced chicken with the cornflour (if using), salt, pepper, five-spice and chilli flakes.
2. Add the chicken to the pan and stir-fry for 5 minutes, until golden and starting to crisp.
3. Add the onion, peppers, garlic and fresh chilli (if using). Stir-fry everything together for another 5–6 minutes, until the chicken is cooked through and the veggies are tender but still have a bite.
4. Taste and adjust the seasoning with extra salt and pepper, if needed. Scatter over chopped spring onions and coriander, if you like, and serve straight from the pan.

SWAPS

→ Swap chicken for tofu or reduced-fat halloumi. Both soak up flavours brilliantly and add a different texture, perfect for a meat-free twist.
→ Swap peppers for tenderstem broccoli or sugar snap peas. They add a fresh crunch and keep it vibrant and colourful.
→ Swap Chinese five-spice for ground cumin and coriander. A warm, earthy combo that changes things up but still packs a flavour punch.

SIDES

+ **Ready-to-wok noodles.** Just heat in the same pan for a couple of minutes.
+ **Microwave basmati or jasmine rice.** Cook in the microwave or add straight to the pan, perfect for soaking up all the flavour.
+ **Pre-washed salad leaves.** Fresh and crunchy on the side, no prep needed.

Chicken Korma Rice

❄ GF **SERVES 4** **CALORIES: 427**

I feel like korma gets a bit of a bad rep sometimes, but this version is a total winner. It's creamy, comforting, and comes together with hardly any effort, just how we like it! I usually fling it all into the pan while sorting the kids' homework, and somehow it still feels like a proper treat at the end of the day. A little rice, a lot of flavour, and no stress – what more do we need?

Spray oil
500g chicken breast, diced
1 small onion, finely chopped
3 tsp garlic purée
2 tbsp korma curry paste
400ml reduced-fat coconut milk
2 tbsp 0% Greek yoghurt
500g cold cooked basmati or pilau rice (I use microwave rice)
A handful of frozen peas
Salt and black pepper, to taste
Chopped fresh coriander or flaked almonds, to garnish (optional)

1. Spray a large pan with oil and cook the chicken over a medium-high heat for 4–5 minutes, until starting to brown.
2. Add the chopped onion and garlic purée, cooking for another 2–3 minutes until softened.
3. Stir in the korma paste and cook for a minute to bring out the flavour, then pour in the coconut milk and give everything a good mix. Simmer for 2 minutes, then stir in the yoghurt, rice, and peas.
4. Heat through for 3–4 minutes, until piping hot and the sauce thickens slightly. Season to taste and serve, sprinkled with chopped coriander or flaked almonds, if you fancy.

SWAPS

→ **Swap chicken breast for prawns.** They cook in minutes and go so well with the creamy korma – just toss them in at the end.

→ **Swap Greek yoghurt for light crème fraîche.** Adds a bit of tang and creaminess, and great if it's already in the fridge.

→ **Swap basmati rice for cauliflower rice.** A lighter, low-carb option that still soaks up every bit of that sauce.

SIDES

+ **Naan bread.** Warm it in the toaster, grill or air fryer and dunk away, so easy and so satisfying.
+ **Crispy poppadoms.** No prep needed, just open the packet and scoop up that curry.
+ **Cucumber and mint raita.** Light, cooling and ready in seconds, perfect with the rich korma and adds a lovely fresh crunch.

Cheeseburger Pasta

SERVES 4 **CALORIES: 610**

This is one of those dinners that tastes like a total guilty pleasure, but it's surprisingly simple and quick. Fresh pasta means no waiting around, and everything gets tossed into one big cheesy, beefy hug of a dish. The kids demolish it. I usually make extra, and somehow it still disappears.

Spray oil
500g lean 5% beef mince
1 small onion, finely chopped
3 tsp garlic purée
2 tbsp tomato purée
2 tbsp ketchup
2 tbsp American mustard
500ml hot beef stock
500g fresh pasta (penne or fusilli work well)
100g light cream cheese
80g extra mature Cheddar, grated
Salt and black pepper, to taste

TO SERVE
Burger sauce, for drizzling
Chopped gherkins or spring onions (optional)

1. Spray a large pan with oil and place over a medium to high heat. Add the mince and onion, breaking up the meat with a spoon, and cook for 3–4 minutes, until browned.
2. Stir in the garlic purée, tomato purée, ketchup and mustard, and cook for 1 minute. Pour in the hot beef stock and bring to a simmer. Add the fresh pasta, cover with a lid or foil, and cook for 4–5 minutes, until the pasta is tender (check the timing on the packet).
3. Stir through the cream cheese and Cheddar until the sauce is thick and glossy. Season to taste. Top with a drizzle of burger sauce and your favourite toppings, such as chopped gherkins or spring onions.

SWAPS

→ **Swap beef mince for turkey mince.** A leaner choice that still gives that meaty base.
→ **Swap fresh pasta for dried pasta.** Just cook it for longer and increase the stock to 800ml–1 litre.
→ **Swap cream cheese for low-fat crème fraîche.** Still gives you a creamy finish with a tangy twist.

SIDES

+ **Side salad with pickles.** Adds crunch and freshness without extra cooking.
+ **Toasted burger buns or brioche fingers.** Hear me out, perfect for scooping or just making it feel more 'burger-y'.
+ **Microwave green beans or peas.** For a quick and easy bit of green on the side.

Lamb Doner Kebabs

SERVES 4 **CALORIES: 535**

I started making this on a whim one Friday night when we were craving a kebab but didn't fancy spending £30 on a takeaway. It's now a full-on family ritual. Everyone gets involved – someone warms the pittas, someone else builds the salad, and I'm on kebab-slicing duty. It's quick, tasty and always hits the spot.

Spray oil
500g lean 5% lamb mince
1 small onion, grated
1 tsp garlic granules
1 tsp onion granules
1 tsp ground cumin
1 tsp ground coriander
1 tsp smoked paprika
½ tsp ground cinnamon
½ tsp salt
½ tsp black pepper

FOR THE GARLIC YOGHURT MAYO
2 heaped tbsp 0% Greek yoghurt
2 heaped tbsp light mayo
1 tsp garlic purée or 1 small garlic clove, crushed
A squeeze of lemon juice
Salt and black pepper, to taste

TO SERVE
4 wholemeal or white pittas
Shredded lettuce
Sliced cucumber
Sliced red onion
Cherry tomatoes, halved

1. Preheat your grill to high. Line a tray with foil and lightly spray it with oil.
2. In a bowl, mix together the lamb mince, grated onion, garlic granules, onion granules, cumin, coriander, paprika, cinnamon, salt and black pepper.
3. Use your hands or a food processor to mix until well combined. Shape the mixture into a large, flat rectangle or oval (about 2cm thick) on the tray. Pop under the grill for 10–12 minutes, turning halfway, until golden and cooked through.
4. While it's grilling, mix together all the garlic yoghurt mayo ingredients in a small bowl. Warm your pittas (grill, or toaster), then slice the cooked lamb into thin strips.
5. Stuff the pittas with salad, lamb and a good drizzle of the garlic mayo.

SWAPS

→ **Swap lamb mince for beef or turkey mince.** Still delicious and can reduce fat slightly if using leaner cuts.
→ **Swap garlic mayo for tzatziki.** Fresher, zingier and a bit lighter, great with the spices.
→ **Swap pittas for flatbreads or tortilla wraps.** Use whatever's in the cupboard, great for kids to make their own wraps, too.

SIDES

+ **Ready-made couscous salad.** Grab a box from the supermarket fridge aisle – fresh, filling and no prep.
+ **Store-bought hummus or chilli sauce.** Great for dipping or drizzling, adds an extra layer of flavour.

Thai Red Curry Noodles

SERVES 4 **CALORIES: 335**

Spray oil
2 tsp garlic purée
3 tsp ginger purée
2 tbsp Thai red curry paste
1 small broccoli head, cut into small florets
1 red pepper, thinly sliced
150g sugar snap peas, halved
400ml low-fat coconut milk
600g raw peeled prawns
300g straight-to-wok noodles (rice or egg noodles)
1 tbsp light soy sauce, plus extra to finish (optional)
Juice of 1 lime, plus extra to finish (optional)

TO SERVE
Chopped fresh coriander
Sliced red chilli, for extra heat (optional)

This Thai red curry noodle dish hits all the right notes – creamy, spicy and packed with prawns for a protein punch. It's got just the right kick to keep things interesting without being overpowering, making it a crowd-pleaser for everyone around the table. Plus, it's easy enough to whip up on a busy day but feels like something a bit special.

1. Spray a large deep pan or wok with oil and place over a medium to high heat. Add the garlic purée and ginger purée, and cook for 30 seconds until fragrant. Stir in the red curry paste and cook for 1 minute.
2. Add the broccoli florets, red pepper and sugar snap peas and stir-fry for 1 minute, then pour in the coconut milk and simmer gently for 3 minutes. Add the prawns and noodles, stirring to combine.
3. Add the soy sauce and lime juice, then cover with a lid or foil. Cook for 3–4 minutes, stirring halfway, until the noodles are tender and the prawns are cooked through.
4. Check the seasoning and add more lime juice or soy sauce, if needed. Sprinkle with chopped coriander and sliced chilli if you like a bit of heat, and serve.

SWAPS

→ Swap prawns for tofu or reduced-fat halloumi. A veggie-friendly swap that still packs in the protein and soaks up the curry sauce.

→ Swap sugar snap peas for mangetout or green beans. Keeps the crunch but changes up the texture and flavour a little.

→ Swap Thai red curry paste for mild yellow curry paste. For a gentler, creamier curry if you prefer less heat.

SIDES

+ **Cherry tomatoes, halved.** Sweet and juicy bites that brighten up the dish.
+ **Pickled cucumber or radish slices.** Adds a nice tangy crunch without any fuss.
+ **Toasted nuts or seeds (pre-toasted or store-bought).** Great for adding texture and a little extra protein and fat.

Sweet and Sour Chicken Rice

❄ GF **SERVES 4** **CALORIES: 485**

Spray oil
500g lean chicken breast, diced
1 onion, sliced
1 red pepper, sliced
1 yellow pepper, sliced
2 tsp garlic purée
150g pineapple chunks (fresh or tinned), drained
500g cold cooked basmati rice (I use microwave rice)
150ml pineapple juice (from carton or tinned pineapple)
100ml passata
3 tbsp tomato ketchup
2 tbsp cider vinegar
2 tbsp soy sauce
1 tbsp honey or golden syrup
1 tsp cornflour, mixed with 2 tbsp water (optional, for thickening)
Salt and black pepper, to taste

Sweet and sour chicken always takes me straight back to my childhood – we didn't have takeaways often, so when we did, it felt like the biggest treat. There would always be a fight for the last bit of pineapple, too! This version gives me all those same vibes, but it's speedy, homemade, and the kids now do the fighting instead. Some things never change!

1. Spray a large pan with oil and place over a medium to high heat. Add the diced chicken and cook until sealed all over, about 4 minutes.
2. Toss in the sliced onion, red and yellow peppers, garlic purée and pineapple chunks, and cook for 3 minutes, until softened and warmed through.
3. Stir in the cooked rice, pineapple juice, passata, ketchup, cider vinegar, soy sauce and honey or golden syrup.
4. Mix well, then simmer for 5 minutes, stirring occasionally. If you want a thicker sauce, add the cornflour slurry and cook for 1 more minute, until the sauce thickens.
5. Season with salt and black pepper, and serve.

SWAPS

→ **Swap chicken for pork or turkey.** Still great, with a mild flavour, and cooks quickly.
→ **Swap pineapple juice for orange juice.** Adds a different kind of tangy sweetness.
→ **Swap passata for chopped tomatoes.** For a chunkier texture to the sauce.

SIDES

+ **Steamed greens such as broccoli or tenderstem.** Quick steam or microwave for 3–5 minutes.
+ **Pickled red cabbage or cucumber slices.** To add crunch and tang without cooking.
+ **Ready-to-eat crunchy salad leaves.** Fresh and easy to serve alongside.

Loaded Steak Nachos

GF · **SERVES 4** · **CALORIES: 620**

Spray oil
250g lean rump or sirloin steak, thinly sliced
1 tsp smoked paprika
½ tsp ground cumin
½ tsp garlic granules
Salt and black pepper, to taste
1 red pepper, diced
1 green pepper, diced
1 red onion, finely sliced
200g tortilla chips
100g extra mature Cheddar, grated
100g cherry tomatoes, halved
2 spring onions, sliced
2 tbsp sour cream
2 tbsp salsa
1 tbsp jalapeños (optional)

If there's one way to guarantee that my husband appears in the kitchen sniffing around like he's never been fed, it's the smell of steak and melted cheese. These loaded nachos are dangerously moreish and somehow convince everyone that I've gone all out when really, I've just thrown everything in a pan and hoped for the best. Perfect for movie nights, game nights, or any night when you can't be bothered but still want full brownie points.

1. Spray a large pan with oil and place over a medium to high heat. Toss the steak with the paprika, cumin, garlic granules, salt and black pepper.
2. Add the steak to the pan and sear for 2 minutes, until browned and just cooked through. Remove and set aside. In the same pan, cook the peppers and onion for 3–4 minutes until softened, then pop them aside with the steak.
3. Turn off the heat and spread the tortilla chips directly in the pan. Layer over the steak, peppers and onion. Sprinkle with the grated Cheddar and cover with a lid or foil until the cheese has melted.
4. Top with the cherry tomatoes, spring onions, sour cream, salsa and jalapeños, if you fancy a kick. Dig in straight from the pan, no extra dishes needed!

SWAPS

→ **Swap lean steak for cooked chicken or prawns.** Ideal for using leftovers and keeps things quick.
→ **Swap Cheddar for full-fat mozzarella or Mexican chilli cheese.** Mild and melty or full of fiery flavour, your call.
→ **Swap peppers for sweetcorn or black beans.** A budget-friendly way to bulk it up and add texture.

SIDES

+ **Chunky guacamole.** Store-bought or homemade, it's always a hit.
+ **Crisp lettuce or slaw.** Adds freshness and a nice crunchy contrast.
+ **Pickled onions or gherkins.** Tangy and bold, perfect for cutting through all the cheesiness.

Sticky Chinese Beef Lettuce Wraps

GF · **SERVES 4** · **CALORIES: 418**

1 tsp sesame oil
500g lean 5% beef mince
1 onion, finely diced
2 tsp garlic purée
1 red pepper, finely diced
1 carrot, grated
3 tbsp hoisin sauce
2 tbsp light soy sauce
1 tbsp honey
1 tbsp rice vinegar
½ tsp Chinese five-spice
1 spring onion, finely sliced

TO SERVE
Baby gem lettuce leaves
Sesame seeds and extra spring onions, to garnish

Lettuce... one of those things my kids claim they hate, until it's holding sticky, sweet beef and suddenly it's the best thing ever. These wraps are like a magic trick in our house, quick to make, fun to eat, and they somehow get greens into the kids without a single moan. Everyone builds their own at the table, so there's less fuss and more fun.

1. Heat the sesame oil in a large frying pan or wok over a medium to high heat. Add the beef mince and break it up with a spoon. Cook for 3–4 minutes, until browned.
2. Add the onion, garlic purée, red pepper and grated carrot, and stir-fry for 3–4 minutes until softened. Stir in the hoisin sauce, soy sauce, honey, rice vinegar and five-spice.
3. Let it bubble away for 2–3 minutes, until sticky and glossy. Toss through the spring onions and remove from the heat. Spoon into lettuce cups and sprinkle with sesame seeds and more spring onions.

SWAPS

→ **Swap beef mince for turkey mince.** Lower in fat but still full of flavour.
→ **Swap hoisin for teriyaki sauce.** A little less sweet and gives a lovely glaze.
→ **Swap five-spice for ground ginger.** Different flavour, still brings warmth and depth.

SIDES

+ **Serve with microwave jasmine or basmati rice.** Ready in minutes and perfect for soaking up all that sticky sauce.
+ **Add prawn crackers.** Great for scooping and snacking.
+ **Add sliced cucumber and radishes.** Fresh and crunchy to balance the sticky filling.

Buffalo Chicken Quesadillas

SERVES 4 **CALORIES: 595**

Spray oil
500g chicken breasts, thinly sliced
Salt and black pepper, to taste
1 red onion, finely sliced
2 tsp garlic purée
4 tbsp buffalo hot sauce
2 tbsp cream cheese
3 tbsp ranch dressing
3 spring onions, finely sliced
4 large tortilla wraps
120g extra mature Cheddar, grated

There's something about buffalo sauce that just speaks to my soul. These buffalo ranch quesadillas are messy, cheesy, spicy little pockets of joy that never last long in our house. My daughter Lottie tries to act like they're 'too spicy', but somehow still manages to finish the whole plate. Honestly, these are dangerously moreish, don't say I didn't warn you.

1. Spray the pan lightly with oil and place over a medium heat. Add the sliced chicken and season with salt and black pepper. Cook for 4–5 minutes, until golden and cooked through.
2. Add the red onion and cook for 2–3 minutes, to soften. Stir in the garlic purée and buffalo sauce, then reduce the heat and cook for another 2 minutes until everything is hot and coated.
3. Turn off the heat and stir in the cream cheese, ranch dressing and spring onions. Mix well, then remove from the pan and set aside for now.
4. Wipe out the pan and return it to a medium heat. Place a tortilla wrap in the pan, spoon a quarter of the chicken mixture on to one half, sprinkle with cheese, then fold the other half over.
5. Cook for 2–3 minutes each side, until golden and crispy. Repeat with the remaining wraps. Slice into wedges and serve hot.

SWAPS

→ **Swap chicken for tofu or reduced-fat halloumi.** Cooks quickly and gives a yummy vegetarian twist.
→ **Swap Cheddar for full-fat mozzarella.** For an extra melty cheese-pull moment and fewer calories.
→ **Swap ranch dressing for sour cream.** Tangy and creamy, a great option if ranch isn't your thing.

SIDES

+ **Ready-made coleslaw.** Adds crunch and coolness on the side.
+ **Bagged salad with extra ranch dressing.** Super quick, no chopping required.
+ **Pickled jalapeños or gherkins.** They bring a tangy kick to balance the spice.

Philly Cheese Steak Sub

SERVES 4 **CALORIES: 445**

Spray oil
1 red onion, finely sliced
1 green pepper, finely sliced
500g lean 5% beef mince
2 tsp garlic granules
1 tsp onion granules
1 tsp smoked paprika
Salt and black pepper, to taste
4 white sub rolls
4 full-fat mozzarella slices

SWAPS

→ **Swap mozzarella for light cheese slices.** Cuts a few more calories and still melts beautifully.
→ **Swap beef mince for thinly sliced steak.** For a more authentic, indulgent cheesesteak.
→ **Swap sub rolls for wholemeal wraps.** For a lower-calorie version of the classic.

I'm all about those meals that feel like a warm hug after a crazy day, and this one ticks all the boxes. It's quick, comforting, and just the kind of food that makes you forget the chaos for a bit. Plus, it's one that my kids actually love, which means bonus points for me! Perfect for when you want something easy but still want to feel like you have your life together.

1. Spray a large pan with oil and pop it over a medium heat. Add the sliced red onion and green pepper and cook for around 3 minutes, until softened.
2. Move them to one side of the pan, then add the beef mince and break it up as it cooks. Once the mince is browned, stir in the garlic granules, onion granules, paprika and a good pinch each of salt and black pepper.
3. Let it cook through for another couple of minutes. Grab 4 white sub rolls, slice them open and pop a slice of mozzarella into each one. Spoon in the hot beefy filling while it's still sizzling so that the cheese starts to melt right in, and serve.

SIDES

+ **Sweet potato wedges.** Roasted with spray oil and paprika for a warm, tasty side that's naturally sweet and filling.
+ **Ready-made slaw with light mayo or 0% Greek yoghurt.** Mixed with a splash of vinegar for an easy, fresh crunch.
+ **Tomato, cucumber and feta salad.** Drizzled with olive oil and lemon juice for a fresh, tangy side that's simple but satisfying.

Spicy Szechuan Pork and Green Bean Stir-fry

❄ · GF · **SERVES 4** · **CALORIES: 312**

1 tbsp oil
500g lean 5% pork mince
1 red onion, finely sliced
2 garlic cloves, grated
1 tsp ginger purée
200g green beans, trimmed and halved
2 tsp Chinese five-spice
2 tbsp Szechuan chilli oil, or to taste
3 tbsp light soy sauce
1 tbsp dark soy sauce
1 tbsp rice vinegar
1 tbsp honey
1 tbsp tomato purée
1 tbsp cornflour, mixed with 2 tbsp water
1 spring onion, finely sliced, to serve

If you love a fakeaway with a kick, this one's for you. It's a proper fiery little stir-fry, packed with crispy pork mince, crunchy green beans and loads of bold Szechuan flavours. The sauce is rich, spicy, a bit sticky and totally addictive. No faff, no marinating, just a quick dinner that hits the spot. Perfect on its own, or piled onto rice, noodles or even lettuce cups, if you fancy.

1. Heat the oil in a large pan over a medium to high heat. Add the pork mince and cook for 5–6 minutes, breaking it up until golden and slightly crisp.
2. Stir in the red onion, garlic, ginger purée, green beans and Chinese five-spice. Cook for 2–3 minutes, until the beans start to soften.
3. Add the Szechuan chilli oil, both soy sauces, the rice vinegar, honey and tomato purée. Let it bubble for a minute.
4. Pour in the cornflour slurry and stir until the sauce thickens and coats everything nicely.
5. Serve topped with spring onions and your choice of side (see suggestions!).

SWAPS

→ **Swap pork mince for chicken or turkey mince.** Still juicy and flavour-packed with a lighter twist.
→ **Swap green beans for mangetout or sliced peppers.** Keeps it crunchy but adds a bit of colour.
→ **Swap Szechuan chilli oil for gochujang or sweet chilli.** Adjust the spice level and flavour profile to suit your taste.

SIDES

+ **Serve with cooked basmati or jasmine rice.** Perfect for soaking up all that spicy Szechuan sauce.
+ **Toss through cooked egg noodles.** Turns it into a speedy noodle bowl dinner.
+ **Ladle into lettuce cups for a lighter option.** Fresh, crunchy and great for summer evenings.

Prawn Pad Thai-style Noodles

SERVES 4   **CALORIES: 426**

This is my speedy, one-pan take on a classic Pad Thai, still packed with all the flavour, just made easier for busy nights. Juicy prawns, soft noodles, crunchy veg and that sweet-sour tamarind sauce that ties it all together... it's honestly one of those meals that tastes like a proper treat but takes no time at all. Piled high with peanuts, spring onions and a good squeeze of lime, it's fakeaway vibes without the faff.

1 tbsp oil
3 spring onions, sliced (keep the green bits for garnish)
2 garlic cloves, grated
1 tsp ginger purée
200g cooked king prawns
2 eggs, lightly beaten
2 x 300g packs of straight-to-wok rice noodles
1 large carrot, peeled into ribbons or finely sliced
100g beansprouts
2 tbsp tamarind sauce (or tamarind paste mixed with a little water)
1 tbsp fish sauce
1 tbsp soy sauce
1 tbsp brown sugar
Juice of ½ a lime
1 tbsp peanut butter (optional – helps thicken and mellow the tanginess)
Crushed peanuts and lime wedges, to serve

1. Heat the oil in a large pan over a medium to high heat. Add the white part of the spring onions, garlic and ginger purée, and cook for 1–2 minutes, until fragrant.
2. Add the prawns and cook for 2–3 minutes until heated through. Push everything to the side of the pan and pour in the eggs. Scramble for 1–2 minutes, until just set.
3. Toss in the rice noodles, carrot ribbons and beansprouts. Break up the noodles and mix everything together.
4. Stir in the tamarind sauce, fish sauce, soy sauce, brown sugar, lime juice and peanut butter (if using). Cook for another 1–2 minutes, until everything's glossy and coated.
5. Top with the green bits of the spring onion, crushed peanuts and a squeeze of lime.

SWAPS

→ Swap prawns for tofu or cooked chicken. Easy switch that works just as well with the sauce.
→ Swap tamarind for a mix of lime juice and brown sugar. Handy if you don't have tamarind, but still gives that sweet-sour tang.

SIDES

+ Serve with Thai sweet chilli dipping sauce on the side. Adds a little extra sweetness and spice.
+ Top with sliced red chillies or chilli flakes. For those who like it hot.
+ Add a quick Thai cucumber salad. Refreshing and crunchy next to the rich noodles.

Cheat's Fish and Chips

SERVES 4 **CALORIES: 452**

1 tbsp oil
1 x 560g tin of new potatoes, sliced into ½cm rounds
1 tsp smoked paprika
1 tsp garlic granules
salt and black pepper, to taste
1 tbsp plain flour
½ tsp paprika
4 fresh white fish fillets (e.g. cod or haddock – around 400–500g total)
100g frozen peas
Lemon wedges, to serve (optional)

FOR THE TARTARE SAUCE
4 tbsp light mayo
1 tbsp chopped gherkins
1 tbsp chopped capers
1 tsp Dijon mustard
Juice of ½ a lemon
1 tbsp fresh or dried parsley

This is my cheat's version of fish and chips. We're using sliced tinned potatoes (trust me, they crisp up beautifully!) and fresh fish fillets coated in a quick flour mix for that golden finish. Throw in some peas and a homemade tartare sauce that takes seconds to mix together, and you've got all the chippy vibes without the faff. Perfect for when you fancy comfort food but haven't got time to queue at the chippy.

1. Heat half the oil in a large pan over a medium to high heat. Add the sliced tinned potatoes, paprika, garlic granules, salt and black pepper and fry for 6–8 minutes, turning occasionally, until golden and crispy.
2. Meanwhile, mix the flour with the paprika and ½ teaspoon of salt. Pat the fish fillets dry and lightly coat in the seasoned flour.
3. Push the potatoes to one side of the pan and add a little more oil. Fry the fish fillets for 2–3 minutes each side, until golden and just cooked through.
4. Add the peas to the pan for the last few minutes to heat through.
5. Meanwhile, mix together all the tartare sauce ingredients in a small bowl with a pinch each of salt and pepper.
6. Serve the crispy sliced potatoes with the golden fish, peas and a big spoonful of tartare sauce. Finish with lemon wedges, if you like.

SWAPS

→ Swap cod for basa or haddock. Budget-friendly but still flaky and tender.
→ Swap tinned potatoes for baby potatoes, parboiled and sliced. If you've got a few extra minutes to prep.
→ Swap peas for frozen mixed veg. Easy way to bulk it out and add colour.

SIDES

+ Add pickled onions or beetroot on the side. Proper old-school chip-shop vibes.
+ Serve with buttered bread or a soft roll. For the ultimate fish-and-chip butty.
+ Drizzle with malt vinegar and a pinch of salt. You can't beat that classic finishing touch.

Comfort in a Flash

Cheesy Pork and Tarragon Gnocchi

 SERVES 4 **CALORIES: 535**

Spray oil
500g lean 5% pork mince
1 small onion, finely diced
3 tsp garlic purée
2 tsp dried tarragon (or 2 tbsp fresh)
1 tbsp tomato purée
500g fresh gnocchi
200ml hot chicken stock
300ml passata
80g extra mature Cheddar, grated
30g Parmesan, grated
Salt and black pepper, to taste
Chopped fresh parsley, to finish (optional)

Some nights you want to cook like a pro, and some nights you just want dinner done before anyone asks for snacks again. This cheesy pork mince and tarragon gnocchi is a real winner: zero faff. It's rich, comforting and tastes like you've made an effort (even if you were googling 'what to do with pork mince' ten minutes ago while hiding in the fridge).

1. Spray a large frying pan with oil and place over a medium to high heat. Add the pork mince and cook for 5–6 minutes, breaking it up until golden and starting to crisp.
2. Stir in the onion, garlic purée and tarragon. Cook for 2–3 minutes, until softened. Add the tomato purée and cook for a further minute.
3. Tip in the gnocchi, then pour in the hot chicken stock and passata. Simmer for 3–4 minutes with a lid on until the gnocchi are soft and the sauce has thickened slightly.
4. Stir through the Cheddar and Parmesan until melted and glossy.
5. Season to taste and finish with chopped parsley, if you like.

SWAPS

→ **Swap pork mince for sausage meat.** Adds loads of flavour with zero effort, just squeeze from the skins and cook as normal.
→ **Swap gnocchi for fresh pasta.** Fusilli or penne both work well, just pop them in as you would the gnocchi.
→ **Swap tarragon for mixed herbs or basil.** Whatever's in the cupboard, still gives that herby lift without needing anything fancy.

SIDES

+ **Garlic flatbreads.** Toast or air-fry them, perfect for scooping up all that cheesy sauce.
+ **Ready-to-eat salad leaves.** Go for rocket or baby spinach, no prep, just a handful to balance the richness.
+ **Mini antipasti board.** A few olives, cherry tomatoes and cured meats makes it feel like a treat with no cooking involved.

Spicy Sausage and Pesto Gnocchi

 SERVES 4   **CALORIES: 530**

Spray oil
8 pork sausages, skins removed
1 red onion, finely sliced
2 tsp garlic purée
1 tbsp tomato purée
½ tsp chilli flakes (or to taste)
1 x 400g tin of chopped tomatoes
200ml hot chicken stock
500g fresh gnocchi
3 tbsp green pesto
Salt and black pepper, to taste
80g extra mature Cheddar, grated
Fresh basil, to serve (optional)

Some dinners just hit the spot without you really knowing why, and this is one of those. Spicy sausage, soft gnocchi, a bit of pesto stirred through… it's the kind of meal that feels like a big hug after a long day. It's simple, quick and everyone in our house clears their plates without a word (a rare moment of peace I'll happily take!).

1. Spray a large pan with oil and place over a medium heat. Add the sausage meat, breaking it up as it browns, and cook for 4–5 minutes, until golden.
2. Add the sliced onion and cook for another 2 minutes, until soft.
3. Stir in the garlic purée, tomato purée and chilli flakes, and let it sizzle for a minute.
4. Pour in the chopped tomatoes and hot chicken stock, and bring to a simmer.
5. Stir in the gnocchi and cook for 3–4 minutes, until the sauce thickens slightly and the gnocchi are soft.
6. Turn off the heat, stir through the pesto, season with salt and black pepper, then top with the grated Cheddar and leave until melted and creamy.
7. Tear over some basil leaves, if you like, and serve.

SWAPS

- Swap pork sausages for veggie sausages and chicken stock for veggie stock. Also check the cheese is veggie. Still spicy, still packed with flavour, just plant-based!
- Swap green pesto for red pesto. For a richer, slightly sweeter twist.
- Swap Cheddar for full-fat mozzarella. Gives you that gorgeous, stringy melt with every bite.

SIDES

+ **Quick side salad.** Rocket, cherry tomatoes and balsamic glaze for a zingy contrast.
+ **Garlic bread.** Ready-made, popped into the oven while the sauce simmers.
+ **Steamed green beans or broccoli.** Microwave a bag for 3–4 minutes, for a fresh crunch on the side.

Chicken, Ham and Stuffing Crumble

 SERVES 4   **CALORIES: 496**

Spray oil
1 onion, finely diced
2 garlic cloves, grated
300g cooked chicken, shredded or chopped
150g cooked ham, chopped
100g frozen peas
1 tsp dried thyme
1 tbsp Dijon mustard (optional)
300ml hot chicken stock
100g light cream cheese

FOR THE TOPPING
100g dry stuffing mix
2 tbsp unsalted butter or light spread
50ml boiling water

This is one of those meals that just hits the spot, creamy, comforting and packed with flavour. Tender chicken, salty ham and that golden stuffing crumble on top... Perfect for using up bits in the fridge and when you want something hearty without making a big fuss.

1. Spray a large ovenproof frying pan with oil and place over a medium heat. Add the onion and garlic and cook for 2–3 minutes, until softened.
2. Stir in the cooked chicken, ham and peas. Add the thyme and mustard (if using) and pour in the hot chicken stock. Simmer for 2–3 minutes.
3. Stir in the cream cheese until melted and smooth, then turn off the heat.
4. In a bowl, mix the dry stuffing with the butter and boiling water. Fluff it with a fork until crumbly.
5. Scatter the stuffing over the creamy filling and pop the pan under the grill for 3–5 minutes, until golden and crisp on top.

SWAPS

→ **Swap ham for leftover roast pork or bacon.** Makes use of leftovers and keeps that cosy vibe.
→ **Swap peas for spinach or sweetcorn.** Easy to customise based on what you've got.
→ **Swap cream cheese for garlic and herb cream cheese.** Adds extra flavour without any more effort.

SIDES

+ **Serve with roast carrots or broccoli.** To add colour and keep things balanced.
+ **Dish up with buttery mash or roasties.** Because it's basically a deconstructed roast dinner.
+ **Top with a spoon of cranberry or apple sauce.** Adds sweetness and sharpness that works so well.

Comfort in a Flash

Garlic Butter Chicken Rice

  SERVES 4   **CALORIES: 520**

Spray oil
500g diced chicken breast
30g unsalted butter
1 small onion, finely diced
6 tsp garlic purée
1 tsp dried parsley
1 tsp smoked paprika
Salt and black pepper, to taste
300ml hot chicken stock
500g cold cooked basmati rice (I use microwave rice)
80g extra mature Cheddar, grated
30g Parmesan, grated
Chopped fresh parsley, to serve
Chilli flakes, to serve

This recipe came together because sometimes you just need dinner that's quick, tasty and fuss-free – no overthinking, no fancy ingredients. I love using microwave rice for exactly that reason: it's ready when I am, and it means everything cooks in one pan. Chicken, garlic butter, cheesy goodness – simple, comforting and perfect for those busy nights when you want good food without the hassle.

1. Spray a large pan with oil and place over a medium to high heat. Add the chicken and cook for 4–5 minutes, until starting to brown.
2. Add the butter, onion, garlic purée, parsley, paprika, salt and black pepper. Stir and cook for 2–3 minutes, until fragrant and softened.
3. Pour in the hot chicken stock and bring to a gentle bubble.
4. Stir in the cooked rice and mix everything together well. Cook for 2–3 minutes, to heat it all through.
5. Sprinkle in the Cheddar and Parmesan, pop a lid on until the cheese has melted, then scatter over some chopped parsley and chilli flakes and serve.

SWAPS

→ **Swap chicken breast for thigh.** Juicier and a bit more forgiving if you overcook it.
→ **Swap Cheddar for light cheese.** Still melts well but cuts the calories a bit.
→ **Swap microwave rice for leftover cooked rice.** Perfect way to use up what's in the fridge, just break it up before adding.

SIDES

+ **Steamed green beans or peas.** Cooked in the microwave while the rice finishes, no extra pans needed.
+ **Chopped cherry tomatoes and a leafy salad.** Fresh, crispy and juicy on the side, cuts through the richness.
+ **Ready-made garlic naan.** For a garlicky double hit, tear and scoop straight from the pan.

Creamy Lemon and Garlic Ravioli

SERVES 4 **CALORIES: 495**

Spray oil
1 medium onion, finely chopped
6 tsp garlic purée
Zest and juice of 1 lemon
400ml hot chicken or vegetable stock
250g light cream cheese
Salt and black pepper, to taste
2 x 250g packs of fresh ravioli (I use spinach and ricotta)
2 big handfuls of spinach
4 tbsp grated Parmesan (optional)

Ravioli always feels a bit posh, but let's be honest, I grabbed it at the supermarket while mentally planning packed lunches and wondering if we've got enough milk to survive until morning. This creamy lemon and garlic version is my go-to when I want dinner to taste like I've made an effort, without actually doing much. No complaints from the kids, and my husband asked if there was more, which is basically the dream.

1. Spray a large pan with oil and place over a medium heat. Add the onion and cook for 2–3 minutes, until softened.
2. Stir in the garlic purée and lemon zest, cooking for 1 minute until fragrant.
3. Add the hot stock and cream cheese, stirring until smooth. Squeeze in enough lemon juice to taste, season, and bring to a gentle simmer.
4. Add both packs of ravioli and cook gently for 4–5 minutes, until soft and heated through.
5. Stir in the spinach and let it wilt, then top with the Parmesan, if using. Serve hot, with extra lemon zest and black pepper, if you fancy.

SWAPS

→ **Swap spinach and ricotta ravioli for chicken or mushroom ravioli.** A quick switch to change up the flavour, pick your fave or whatever's on offer.
→ **Swap cream cheese for light mascarpone.** Still creamy and indulgent, just a little richer.
→ **Swap Parmesan for a sprinkle of extra mature Cheddar or Grana Padano.** Whatever hard cheese you've got in the fridge, they all work!

SIDES

+ **Garlic bread.** The kind you just bung in the oven, perfect for scooping up that creamy sauce.
+ **Ready-to-eat salad leaves with balsamic glaze.** No prep, just plate it up for something crisp and sweet on the side.
+ **Steamed green beans or broccoli.** A quick microwave bag does the job and adds a bit of crunch and colour.

Honey Garlic and Chilli Ramen

SERVES 4 **CALORIES: 490**

Spray oil
2 tsp garlic purée
1 tsp ginger purée
2 tbsp soy sauce
1 tbsp honey
1 tsp chilli oil (adjust to taste)
600ml boiling water
1 chicken stock cube
2 portions of dried ramen noodles
2 spring onions, finely sliced
1 medium carrot, grated
150ml single cream (optional)
Sesame seeds, chopped fresh coriander and extra chilli oil, to serve

SWAPS

→ **Swap single cream for 0% Greek yoghurt.** For a tangier, lighter, creamy finish without losing richness.

→ **Swap dried ramen noodles for instant udon.** Thicker noodles for a chewy, satisfying bite.

→ **Swap soy sauce for tamari or coconut aminos.** Great if you want gluten-free or a slightly sweeter twist.

Some days just need a meal that feels like a big, warm hug, and this creamy honey, garlic and chilli ramen is exactly that for me. It's comforting and a little indulgent, and somehow it makes the chaos feel a bit more manageable. Plus, I can whip it up super quickly and sneak in some veg. It's my little way of reminding myself that even when things are hectic, I've still got this.

1. Spray a pan with oil and place over a medium to high heat. Add the garlic purée and ginger purée and cook for 1 minute, until fragrant.
2. Add the soy sauce, honey and chilli oil, stir and let bubble for 30 seconds, then pour in the boiling water. Crumble in the stock cube and stir until dissolved.
3. Add the dried ramen noodles, spring onions and grated carrot, and simmer for 4–5 minutes until the noodles are tender and the broth has slightly reduced.
4. Stir in the cream (if using) and heat through for 1–2 minutes to create a creamy sauce. Serve sprinkled with sesame seeds, chopped coriander and extra chilli oil.

SIDES

+ **Add cooked shredded chicken or leftover rôtisserie chicken.** Stir it in right before adding the cream for extra meaty goodness. Or toss in some cooked prawns for a quick seafood upgrade.
+ **Crunchy cucumber ribbons.** So fresh and cooling, a lovely crunch and contrast to the creamy noodles.
+ **Pre-packaged pickled ginger.** Adds a zesty kick and works perfectly with the Asian flavours.
+ **Steamed tenderstem broccoli.** Quickly steam in the microwave or on the stovetop, a vibrant, nutritious side.

Smoked Fish and Sweetcorn Curry

 GF SERVES 4 CALORIES: 270

Spray oil
1 small onion, finely diced
3 tsp garlic purée
2 tsp ginger purée
2 tsp mild curry powder
½ tsp ground turmeric
1 x 400g tin of sweetcorn
100ml hot chicken or vegetable stock
600g smoked haddock fillets, skin off, cut into chunks
100g frozen peas
2 tbsp 0% Greek yoghurt (optional)
Salt and black pepper, to taste
Chopped fresh coriander or parsley, to serve

SWAPS

→ **Swap smoked haddock for cod or salmon.** Just as tasty and still cooks in minutes.
→ **Add spinach.** Stir in a handful at the end for an easy veg boost.
→ **Skip the yoghurt.** The blended sweetcorn keeps it naturally creamy, but a spoonful of coconut milk works well, too.

I wish I could take credit for this one... but it's actually my brother Isaac's creation (don't tell him I said it's genius or I'll never hear the end of it). It's one of those recipes that sounds a bit odd until you try it – smoky fish, blended sweetcorn in the sauce... but trust me, it just works. Creamy, comforting and full of flavour.

1. Spray a large pan with oil and place over a medium to high heat. Add the onion and cook for 2–3 minutes, until softened.
2. Stir in the garlic purée, ginger purée, curry powder and turmeric and cook for 1 minute, to release all the flavours.
3. Meanwhile, blend the sweetcorn with the hot stock until smooth. Pour it into the pan.
4. Add the smoked haddock and peas, stir gently, then simmer for 6–8 minutes until the fish is cooked through and flakes easily.
5. Stir in the Greek yoghurt (if using), and season to taste with salt and black pepper.
6. Serve hot, sprinkled with fresh herbs and with your choice of sides.

SIDES

+ **Steamed basmati rice.** Fluffy, simple and perfect for soaking up the curry sauce.
+ **Warm naan or flatbreads.** For scooping, swiping and wiping the bowl clean – no judgement here.
+ **Cucumber salad.** Crisp, cooling and a great contrast to the smoky, creamy curry.

Honey Mustard Sausage Baguette

SERVES 4 **CALORIES: 518**

Spray oil
6 thin pork sausages (or chipolatas), chopped into bite-size pieces
1 small onion, finely sliced
3 tsp garlic purée
2 tbsp wholegrain mustard
1 tbsp Dijon mustard
2 tbsp honey
30g light cream cheese
Salt and black pepper, to taste (optional)
2 medium baguettes
60g extra mature Cheddar, grated

Let's be honest, some days I want a dinner that feels like I made an effort... but that doesn't require me to *actually* make much effort. Enter these honey mustard sausage baguettes. Sweet, sticky, cheesy and so ridiculously easy, the sausages are even chopped so they cook faster (because I am absolutely not waiting 20 minutes for a sausage to brown). It tastes like you've pulled off something way more impressive than you actually have. Perfect for busy nights or when you just can't face standing in the kitchen for hours.

SWAPS

→ **Swap sausages for cooked chicken.** Great for using up leftovers and still so tasty.
→ **Swap Cheddar for low-fat cheese slices.** Still melty, but saves a few calories.
→ **Swap baguettes for soft tortilla wraps.** Quick, easy and freezer-friendly.

1. Spray a large pan with oil and place over a medium to high heat. Add the chopped sausages and cook for 5–6 minutes, stirring often, until browned all over and cooked through.
2. Add the onion and cook for another 2–3 minutes, until soft.
3. Stir in the garlic purée, both mustards, the honey, cream cheese, and a pinch of salt and black pepper, if needed. Bubble everything together for 1 minute until thick and sticky.
4. Cut the baguettes in half, then slice them open and stuff with the sticky sausage mix. Pop them back into the pan and sprinkle over the cheese. Work in batches if necessary.
5. Cover the pan with a lid or foil and let the cheese melt for 2–3 minutes, then serve.

SIDES

+ **Crisps or baked potato wedges.** Low-effort, no fuss, just grab or reheat.
+ **Bagged salad with balsamic glaze.** A quick, zingy side that cuts through the richness.
+ **Microwaved corn on the cob.** Butter it, salt it, done in minutes.

Creamy Garlic and Herb Lasagne

SERVES 4 **CALORIES: 510**

Spray oil
1 small onion, finely diced
3 tsp garlic purée
2 tsp dried mixed herbs
Salt and black pepper, to taste
300ml hot chicken or vegetable stock
300g fresh lasagne sheets, sliced into strips
400g cooked rôtisserie chicken, shredded
100g garlic and herb cream cheese
80g extra mature Cheddar, grated
A handful of fresh parsley, chopped (optional)

If you love lasagne but hate waiting forever for dinner, this one's for you. It's not fancy or traditional, but it's loaded with all the creamy, garlicky goodness that makes you feel like you've just wrapped yourself in a warm, cheesy hug. Perfect for when you want all those comforting vibes without any fuss.

1. Spray a large pan with oil and place over a medium to high heat. Add the onion and cook for 3–4 minutes, until softened.
2. Add the garlic purée, herbs, salt and black pepper, then pour in the hot stock.
3. Stir in the sliced lasagne sheets and simmer for 4–5 minutes, stirring occasionally.
4. Add the cooked chicken and cream cheese and stir until creamy and coated.
5. Sprinkle over the Cheddar, pop a lid on to let it melt, and finish with fresh parsley.

SWAPS

→ **Swap rôtisserie chicken for Quorn pieces or cooked lentils**, and chicken stock for veggie. Quorn keeps it chunky and satisfying, and lentils are a hearty, budget-friendly option.
→ **Swap fresh lasagne sheets for gnocchi.** No boiling needed, and makes a pillowy, creamy bake that's still one-pot magic.
→ **Swap garlic and herb cream cheese and Cheddar for plant-based versions.** Still rich and creamy, but perfect for keeping it veggie or dairy-free.

SIDES

+ **Crispy garlic bread.** Pop it into the oven while the lasagne simmers – you can't beat a crunchy side to scoop it up with.
+ **Griddled courgettes or aubergine.** Smoky, soft veg that balance the creamy pasta beautifully.
+ **Rocket salad with lemon dressing.** Fresh, peppery and zesty, a lovely contrast to the cheesy sauce.

Tuscan Chicken and Chorizo Beans

  SERVES 4 **CALORIES: 527**

Spray oil
400g chicken breast, diced
150g chorizo, sliced
1 onion, finely chopped
3 tsp garlic purée
2 tsp smoked paprika
1 tsp dried oregano
1 x 400g tin of cannellini beans, drained and rinsed
1 x 400g tin of chopped tomatoes
100ml hot chicken stock
75g light cream cheese
A handful of fresh spinach
Salt and black pepper, to taste
Chopped fresh parsley, to serve

SWAPS

→ **Swap chicken breast for raw peeled prawns.** Quick-cooking and adds a lovely seafood twist.
→ **Swap chorizo for smoky sausage or bacon.** For a milder, less spicy kick.
→ **Swap cannellini beans for butter beans.** For a creamier texture that's just as tasty.

Some recipes are planned. This one was a 'what's in the fridge and how fast can I eat it?' situation. A pack of chicken, a lonely chorizo and a tin of beans later... this beauty was born. It's smoky, creamy, a little spicy, and totally hits the spot when you're tired, hungry, and not in the mood for faff.

1. Spray a large pan with oil and place over a medium to high heat. Add the chicken and chorizo and cook for 3–4 minutes, stirring occasionally, until the chicken is golden and almost cooked through.
2. Add the onion, garlic purée, paprika and oregano. Cook for 2 minutes, until fragrant and the onion has softened.
3. Stir in the cannellini beans, tinned tomatoes and the hot chicken stock. Bring to a simmer, then reduce the heat and cook for 5 minutes, to thicken slightly.
4. Stir in the light cream cheese until melted and creamy.
5. Toss in the spinach and stir until wilted. Season with salt and black pepper.
6. Sprinkle over the parsley and serve straight from the pot.

SIDES

+ **Crusty bread.** Perfect for mopping up all the saucy goodness.
+ **Simple green salad.** Light and fresh to balance the rich flavours.
+ **Roasted new potatoes.** For a comforting, hearty side.

Quick Souvlaki Rice

GF | **SERVES 4** | **CALORIES: 515**

Spray oil
500g diced chicken breast
4 tsp garlic purée
1 tsp dried oregano
½ tsp ground cumin
Zest and juice of 1 lemon
Salt and black pepper, to taste
250g cherry tomatoes, halved
500g cold cooked basmati rice (I use microwave rice)
½ a red onion, thinly sliced
100ml hot chicken stock
60g feta, crumbled
3 tbsp tzatziki (shop-bought or homemade)
A handful of fresh parsley or mint, chopped
Optional extras: sliced cucumber, black olives, extra lemon wedges

I absolutely love making this whenever I'm craving those chilled, relaxed, Greek holiday vibes, without the hassle of packing bags and airport queues! It's like a little trip to the sunshine right in my kitchen.

1. Spray a large pan with oil and place over a medium to high heat. Add the chicken and cook for 4–5 minutes, until browned.
2. Stir in the garlic purée, oregano, cumin, lemon zest and juice, salt and black pepper, and cook for 1 more minute.
3. Add the cherry tomatoes and cook for 2 minutes, until they begin to soften.
4. Stir in the rice, red onion and hot chicken stock. Cook for 3–4 minutes, until everything is piping hot and well combined.
5. Remove from the heat and serve, topped with crumbled feta, dollops of tzatziki, chopped herbs and any extras you fancy, such as cucumber, olives or lemon wedges.

SWAPS

→ **Swap chicken breast for falafel or grilled reduced-fat halloumi, and chicken stock for veggie.** Still gives you that lovely golden bite with all the flavour and makes it totally veggie.

→ **Swap feta for full-fat mozzarella.** A milder option that still adds creaminess without overpowering the dish.

→ **Swap tzatziki for plain 0% Greek yoghurt with garlic and a squeeze of lemon.** A super quick alternative if you don't have tzatziki, still cooling and creamy!

SIDES

+ **Mini flatbreads or warmed pittas.** Perfect for scooping up the rice and tzatziki, feels a bit more hands-on and fun, especially for sharing.
+ **Grilled reduced-fat halloumi slices.** Golden, salty and crisp on the outside, add them on top or on the side for a satisfying bite.

Comfort in a Flash

Smoked Sausage and Sweet Potato Hash

  SERVES 4 **CALORIES: 448**

Spray oil
500g sweet potatoes, peeled and diced small
400g smoked sausage (e.g. Mattessons), sliced
1 red onion, finely sliced
1 red pepper, diced
2 tsp smoked paprika
1 tsp garlic granules
Salt and black pepper, to taste
100g spinach
1 tbsp honey (optional)
1 tsp chilli oil (optional)
Chopped fresh parsley or spring onions, to finish (optional)

I made this on one of those evenings when everyone was hungry and I hadn't planned a thing. Threw it all into a pan and hoped for the best, and the kids actually loved it (which never usually happens when sweet potatoes are involved!). It's smoky, a bit sweet, a little spicy if you want it, and ready in 15. One pan, no faff, and barely any washing up. Winner.

1. Spray a large pan with oil and place over a medium heat. Add the diced sweet potato and cook for 6–8 minutes, stirring occasionally, until starting to soften and brown.
2. Add the sliced smoked sausage, red onion and red pepper and cook for another 4–5 minutes, until everything is golden and softened.
3. Add the paprika, garlic granules, salt and black pepper, and stir to coat everything in the flavours.
4. Add the spinach along with the honey and the chilli oil (if using). Stir through and cook for 1–2 minutes, until the spinach has wilted and everything is hot.
5. Finish with chopped parsley or spring onions, if you like, and then serve.

SWAPS

→ Swap smoked sausage for chorizo or chicken sausages. Still smoky and full of flavour.
→ Swap sweet potatoes for baby potatoes or butternut squash. Keeps the hash vibe but changes up the texture.
→ Swap spinach for frozen peas or kale. Whatever greens you've got to hand.

SIDES

+ **Top with a fried or poached egg.** That runny yolk with the smoky hash is unreal.
+ **Add a splash of hot sauce.** If you like it spicy, this takes it up a level.
+ **Serve with crusty bread or toasted pittas.** Perfect for scooping it all up.

Pasta in a Pan

Smoked Sausage and Pepper Tortellini

SERVES 4 **CALORIES: 494**

Spray oil
250g smoked sausage, sliced
1 onion, finely sliced
2 mixed peppers, sliced
3 tsp garlic purée
1 tsp smoked paprika
1 tbsp tomato purée
200ml hot chicken stock
150ml single cream
500g fresh tortellini (I use tomato and mozzarella)
Salt and black pepper, to taste
80g extra mature Cheddar or full-fat mozzarella, grated
Chopped fresh parsley or chives, to serve (optional)

This one reminds me of the kind of dinner my mum would've made on a Friday night, something warm, filling and guaranteed to get everyone to the table without a fuss. It's packed with smoky sausage, soft peppers and cheesy tortellini, and it just has that proper comforting feel to it. My lot love it, and I always end up stealing a few bites straight from the pan before it even hits the plates.

1. Spray a large pan with oil and place over a medium heat. Add the sliced sausage and fry for 3–4 minutes, until golden.
2. Add the onion and peppers and cook for 3–4 minutes, until softened. Stir in the garlic purée, smoked paprika and tomato purée and cook for another minute.
3. Pour in the hot chicken stock and single cream, then add the tortellini. Simmer for 3–4 minutes, stirring gently, until the pasta is tender and the sauce has thickened slightly, then season to taste.
4. Sprinkle over the cheese, pop a lid on until melted, and finish with chopped herbs, if you like.

SWAPS

→ **Swap smoked sausage for chicken sausage.** Still meaty and seasoned, but lower in fat and calories.
→ **Swap the tortellini for spinach and ricotta tortellini.** Keeps the cheese vibe and sneaks in some veg.
→ **Swap single cream for light cream cheese.** Trims calories without losing creaminess.

SIDES

+ **Toasted garlic ciabatta slices.** Quick to toast and brilliant for soaking up that creamy sauce.
+ **Charred broccoli florets with chilli and lemon.** Adds crunch, a citrusy hit, and balance to the dish.
+ **Simple tomato and basil salad.** Fresh and vibrant with minimal prep, just vine tomatoes, basil, olive oil and seasoning.

Cheesy Pea and Pesto Pasta

 SERVES 4 **CALORIES: 480**

Spray oil
4 tsp garlic purée
300g dried pasta (fusilli and penne work well)
600ml vegetable stock
150g frozen peas
100g light cream cheese
2 tbsp green pesto
60g extra mature Cheddar, grated
Salt and black pepper, to taste
Extra grated cheese and chopped fresh basil, to serve (optional)

SWAPS

→ **Swap cream cheese for single cream.** Slightly lighter, but still rich and smooth.
→ **Swap Cheddar for full-fat mozzarella or veggie Parmesan.** Adjusts the flavour depending on your mood.
→ **Swap peas for spinach, courgettes or green beans.** A great way to switch up the greens.

This one's as simple as it gets, but still tastes like proper comfort food. Cheesy, garlicky, packed with peas and finished with a big spoonful of pesto, it's creamy, quick and everyone always goes back for seconds. Perfect for those nights when you just want to throw everything into a pan and not think too much about it.

1. Spray a large pan with oil and place over a medium heat. Add the garlic purée and cook for 1 minute, until fragrant.
2. Stir in the pasta and pour in the hot stock. Simmer uncovered for 10–12 minutes, stirring often, until the pasta is tender and most of the liquid has been absorbed.
3. Add the frozen peas during the last 3–4 minutes of the cooking time.
4. Lower the heat, then stir through the cream cheese, pesto and Cheddar until everything is melted, creamy and well combined.
5. Season to taste with salt and black pepper. Top with extra cheese, sprinkle with chopped basil, if you fancy, and serve straight from the pan.

SIDES

+ **Serve with garlic bread or cheesy flatbread.** Ideal for mopping up the sauce.
+ **Add a lemon-dressed salad.** Brightens the dish and cuts through the richness.
+ **Top with pine nuts or crushed toasted almonds.** Adds crunch and a bit of flair.

Crispy Chorizo and 'Nduja Pasta

SERVES 4 **CALORIES: 589**

Spray oil
100g diced chorizo
1 small onion, finely diced
3 tsp garlic purée
1 tbsp 'nduja paste
1 tbsp tomato purée
300ml hot chicken stock
500g fresh pasta (tagliatelle or fusilli work well)
100ml single cream
40g Parmesan, grated
Salt and black pepper, to taste
Fresh basil or parsley, to serve (optional)

SWAPS

→ **Swap fresh pasta for dried pasta.** Just simmer it a bit longer with extra stock, same great flavour.
→ **Swap chorizo for chicken sausage.** Still smoky and savoury, but a bit lighter and more protein.
→ **Add baby spinach.** Wilts down right at the end and adds a little green goodness with no fuss.

This one's a proper flavour bomb – spicy, creamy, rich and just a little bit indulgent (okay, a lot). The first time I made it, my husband walked in and said, 'What smells insanely good?' Then hovered over the pan like a seagull. The combo of crispy chorizo and 'nduja with that silky cream sauce is just unreal. It feels like something you'd order in a restaurant, but it's ready in 15 without leaving the house, which basically makes it perfect in my book.

1. Spray a large non-stick pan with oil and place over a medium heat. Add the chorizo and cook for 3–4 minutes, until crispy. Remove half and set aside.
2. Add the onion and garlic purée to the pan. Cook for 2 minutes until softened, then stir in the 'nduja paste and tomato purée.
3. Pour in the hot chicken stock and bring to a simmer. Add the fresh pasta and cook for 3–4 minutes, stirring often, until just tender.
4. Once the pasta is cooked, stir in the cream and Parmesan. Let it bubble for 1–2 minutes, until the sauce thickens slightly.
5. Season to taste, then top with the reserved crispy chorizo and a sprinkle of herbs, if you like, and serve.

SIDES

+ **Cheesy garlic flatbreads.** Quick to grill and perfect for scooping up any extra sauce.
+ **Roasted Mediterranean veg.** Think courgettes, peppers and red onions, for colour, texture and a bit of balance.
+ **Tomato and mozzarella salad.** Fresh and creamy with a little balsamic, a great contrast to the rich, spicy pasta.

Creamy Harissa and Halloumi Orzo

 V   **SERVES 4**   **CALORIES: 496**

Spray oil
225g reduced-fat halloumi, cut into small cubes
1 small onion, finely diced
3 tsp garlic purée
1 tbsp rose harissa paste
1 tbsp tomato purée
300g dried orzo
700ml hot vegetable stock
100g light cream cheese
2 large handfuls of fresh spinach
Salt and black pepper, to taste
Chopped fresh parsley or mint, to serve (optional)

This one came about on a busy weekday evening, you know the kind where you've barely got time to think, let alone cook? I had some orzo, a bit of harissa and a block of halloumi left in the fridge and Harry (who loves anything with a bit of spice) asked if I could make something 'creamy but with a kick'. So, I threw a few bits together and hoped for the best… and it ended up being one of his favourites!

1. Spray a large pan with oil and place over a medium heat. Add the halloumi and fry for 1–2 minutes, until lightly golden. Remove half and set aside for topping later.
2. Add the onion and garlic purée to the pan and cook for 2 minutes, until soft. Stir in the harissa paste and tomato purée.
3. Add the orzo and the hot stock. Stir well, bring to a simmer, and cook for 8–10 minutes, stirring regularly, until the orzo is tender and most of the liquid has been absorbed.
4. Stir in the cream cheese and spinach, and let it bubble for another minute, until the spinach wilts and the sauce is thick and creamy.
5. Season to taste, then top with the reserved halloumi and a sprinkle of fresh herbs, if you like.

SWAPS

→ **Swap halloumi for diced chicken breast.** A leaner, high-protein option that still pairs perfectly with the creamy sauce.
→ **Swap spinach for courgette ribbons.** Light, fresh and they add a bit of bite – just toss them in for the last couple of minutes.
→ **Swap harissa for red pesto.** Still brings that punchy flavour and colour, but with a sweeter, less spicy finish.

SIDES

+ **Warm flatbreads or pittas.** Perfect for scooping up the creamy orzo and halloumi.
+ **Simple cucumber and mint salad.** Cool, refreshing and balances the spicy harissa.
+ **Roasted cherry tomatoes with thyme.** Adds sweetness, colour and a juicy contrast to the richness.

Red Pesto Beef Pasta

SERVES 4 **CALORIES: 563**

Spray oil
500g lean 5% beef mince
1 small onion, finely diced
3 tsp garlic purée
1 tbsp tomato purée
4 tbsp reduced-fat red pesto
400ml hot chicken stock
500g fresh pasta (penne or fusilli work well)
120g extra mature Cheddar, grated
Salt and black pepper, to taste
Chopped fresh parsley, to serve

This one's a proper weeknight winner. It's rich, cheesy and packed with flavour, but still quick enough to throw together when you're absolutely done in. The red pesto gives it loads of depth, and the beef and Cheddar make it feel like a proper comfort meal. My lot always go back for seconds, and if there's ever any left (rare), it's amazing cold the next day, too.

1. Spray a large pan with oil and place over a medium heat. Add the beef mince and cook for 4–5 minutes, until browned.
2. Stir in the onion and garlic purée and cook for another 2–3 minutes until softened. Add the tomato purée and cook for 1 minute.
3. Stir in the red pesto and the hot chicken stock. Add the fresh pasta and cook for 3–4 minutes, stirring often, until the pasta is tender and coated in the sauce.
4. Sprinkle over the Cheddar and pop a lid on for 2 minutes until it melts. Season to taste and finish with chopped fresh parsley.

SWAPS

→ **Swap beef mince for chicken mince, or for Quorn mince and veg stock if you want it veggie.** Lighter but still full of flavour, perfect if you want to change things up.

→ **Swap Cheddar for full-fat mozzarella.** For a super-melty finish and a yummy cheese pull.

→ **Swap red pesto for sun-dried tomato paste.** Still rich and punchy, fewer calories, works brilliantly.

SIDES

+ **Parmesan-roasted tenderstem broccoli.** Crispy, salty and packed with flavour, adds crunch and a little green without feeling too 'healthy'.
+ **Balsamic roasted veg.** Peppers, courgettes and red onion, adds colour and balance.
+ **Charred corn and tomato salad.** Sweet, smoky and zingy, gives freshness and a pop of colour to balance the richness of the pasta.

Pepperoni and Pesto Orzo

 SERVES 4 **CALORIES: 577**

150g lean diced bacon
80g pepperoni (about 20 slices)
1 red onion, finely diced
2 tsp garlic purée
1 tbsp tomato purée
1 tbsp dried oregano
4 tbsp reduced-fat red pesto
300g dried orzo
700ml hot chicken stock
120g full-fat mozzarella, torn or grated
Salt and black pepper, to taste
Chopped fresh parsley and chilli flakes, to finish (optional)

Lottie came home from school *starving* and asked if we could have 'something like pasta, but also pizza' for dinner, as you do. So, I raided the fridge, found some pepperoni, a bit of pesto and orzo and this dish was born. It's everything she loves in one pan – cheesy, cosy, and packed with flavour. It takes no time at all to throw together, which is always a win on busy weeknights when everyone's got different places to be. Safe to say it's become one of her most-requested dinners... and I'm not complaining.

SWAPS

→ **Swap bacon for turkey bacon.** Cuts calories and fat but keeps the smoky flavour.
→ **Swap pepperoni for chorizo slices.** Adds a spicy, smoky kick with a bit more depth.
→ **Swap full-fat mozzarella for reduced-fat mozzarella.** Keeps it cheesy but cuts some calories.

1. Pop a large pan over a medium to high heat and fry the diced bacon and half the pepperoni for a minute, until crispy and golden. Add the red onion and cook for a minute until soft, then stir in the garlic purée and tomato purée. Let it cook for 30 seconds.
2. Next, sprinkle in the oregano and stir in the pesto. Add the dried orzo and pour over the hot chicken stock. Give everything a good mix, bring to a gentle boil, then reduce the heat and simmer for around 10–11 minutes, stirring now and then, until the orzo is cooked and the sauce is glossy and creamy.
3. Stir in half the mozzarella and season to taste. Top with the rest of the cheese and pepperoni, then pop the whole pan under the grill for 2–3 minutes until bubbling and golden on top. Finish with some chopped parsley and chilli flakes if you fancy, and dig in!

SIDES

+ **Roasted Mediterranean vegetables.** Think courgettes, peppers and aubergines – toss in some herbs and roast while you cook the orzo.
+ **Crispy kale chips.** Quick to make, adds a satisfying crunch and a hit of greens.
+ **Simple 0% Greek yoghurt with lemon and herbs.** A cool, creamy dollop to balance the rich, cheesy orzo.

Roasted Red Pepper and Sausage Pasta

SERVES 4 **CALORIES: 486**

Spray oil
6 pork sausages, sliced (approx. 400g)
1 small onion, finely diced
3 tsp garlic purée
1 tsp smoked paprika
1 tbsp tomato purée
300g roasted red peppers from a jar, drained
300ml hot chicken stock
500g fresh pasta (tagliatelle or fusilli work well)
100ml single cream
30g Parmesan, grated
Salt and black pepper, to taste
Chopped fresh basil or parsley, to serve (optional)

This is one of those dinners that feels a bit fancy but takes zero brainpower to throw together. It's packed with flavour, the sausages make it super hearty, and the creamy roasted pepper sauce is just unreal. Honestly, it's the kind of meal I turn to when I want something really tasty but can't be bothered to think too hard. Everyone in our house loves it, and there are never any leftovers.

1. Spray a large pan with oil and place over a medium heat. Add the sliced sausages and fry for 4–5 minutes, until golden and cooked through.
2. Stir in the onion and garlic purée and cook for 2–3 minutes, until soft. Add the smoked paprika and tomato purée and cook for 1 minute.
3. Meanwhile, blend the roasted red peppers with the hot chicken stock until smooth. Pour into the pan.
4. Add the fresh pasta and cook for 3–4 minutes, stirring often so it soaks up the sauce.
5. Stir in the single cream and Parmesan, letting it bubble for 1–2 minutes until the sauce is rich and glossy.
6. Season to taste and finish with chopped herbs, if you like.

SWAPS

→ **Swap pork sausages for chicken sausages.** Fewer calories but still juicy and flavourful.
→ **Swap roasted peppers for charred aubergine cubes.** Smoky and soft, same texture and adds a different veggie twist.
→ **Swap single cream for light cream cheese.** Keeps it indulgently creamy but with fewer calories.

SIDES

+ **Garlic flatbread.** Soft, buttery and perfect for dipping into every last drop of sauce.
+ **Mixed leaf salad with lemon and olive oil dressing.** Adds fresh crunch and a zingy lift to balance the richness.
+ **Oven-roasted cherry tomatoes.** Sweet, juicy and bursting with extra colour and flavour.

Creamy Garlic and Herb Bacon Ravioli

SERVES 4 **CALORIES: 589**

Spray oil

8 rashers of smoked bacon, chopped

1 small onion, finely diced

3 tsp garlic purée

300ml hot chicken stock

500g fresh ravioli (cheese or spinach work well)

150g garlic and herb cream cheese (I like Boursin)

Black pepper, to taste

Chopped fresh parsley and chives, to serve (optional)

I'm obsessed with garlic and herb cream cheese (Boursin is my go-to), and it works so well stirred into this creamy, indulgent ravioli dish. It's the ultimate lazy-but-feels-fancy dinner – rich, comforting, and so easy it practically cooks itself. It's one of those meals where everyone at the table goes quiet, and if you manage to get the last spoonful, you're winning at life.

1. Spray a large pan with oil and place over a medium heat. Add the bacon and cook for 4–5 minutes, until golden and crisp.
2. Add the onion and garlic purée and cook for 2–3 minutes, until softened.
3. Pour in the hot chicken stock and bring to a simmer. Add the ravioli and cook for 3–4 minutes, stirring gently until tender.
4. Turn off the heat and stir through the garlic and herb cream cheese until melted and creamy. Season with black pepper and top with chopped herbs, if you like.

SWAPS

→ **Swap bacon for pancetta or prosciutto.** Adds a saltier, crispier finish with a bit of Italian flair.

→ **Swap garlic and herb cream cheese for soft cheese.** Same vibe, slightly lighter, ideal if you're watching calories but still want that creamy flavour.

→ **Use mushroom or butternut squash ravioli instead of cheese or spinach.** Adds a bit more depth or sweetness depending on what you fancy.

SIDES

+ **Crispy garlic ciabatta slices.** Crunchy and perfect for dipping into every creamy, cheesy bite.
+ **Pea, mint and lemon salad.** Bright, fresh and with a zing that cuts through the richness.
+ **Crispy sage and butter green beans.** Quick to pan-fry, with a savoury, herby crunch that works beautifully with creamy pasta.

Tuna Crunch Pasta Salad

SERVES 4   **CALORIES: 410**

300g dried pasta (I use conchiglie)
1 red pepper, finely diced
½ a cucumber, diced
2 spring onions, sliced
2–3 gherkins, finely chopped (optional)
1 x 145g tin of sweetcorn, drained
60g extra mature Cheddar, grated
1 x 198g tin of tuna in spring water, drained
3 tbsp light mayo
1 tbsp 0% Greek yoghurt
1 tsp Dijon mustard
Salt and black pepper, to taste

TO SERVE
Crushed tortilla crisps, for topping (optional)
Chopped fresh parsley, squeeze of lemon (optional)

SWAPS

→ **Swap tuna for grilled chicken breast.** Keeps it lean and protein-packed, with a slightly different texture.

→ **Swap Cheddar for crumbled feta.** Adds a nice salty tang and cuts calories a bit.

→ **Swap crushed tortilla crisps for roasted chickpeas.** Still crunchy, but more fibre and a little quicker if you've got a tin in the cupboard.

This one's an absolute hit with my two, which is saying something, because they don't agree on much when it comes to... well, anything really. It's my go-to for lunchboxes, picnics, or when I just need to stop them asking for snacks every ten minutes. It's crunchy, cheesy, tuna-y (is that a word?), and somehow tastes even better when you eat it straight from the pan at the kitchen counter. No judgement here.

1. Cook the pasta in a large pan of salted boiling water according to the packet instructions (around 10–12 minutes).
2. While the pasta cooks, get everything else prepped: chop the veg, grate the cheese, drain the tuna, and crush the crisps if you're using them.
3. Once the pasta's done, drain it and rinse under cold water to cool it down quickly. Pop it back into the pan.
4. Add the tuna, red pepper, cucumber, spring onion, gherkins (if using), sweetcorn and Cheddar to the pasta.
5. Stir through the mayo, yoghurt and Dijon mustard. Season with salt and black pepper and give it a good mix. Sprinkle over the chopped parsley and lemon juice, if using.
6. Top with crushed tortilla crisps just before serving, for extra crunch.

SIDES

+ **Bagged mixed leaves with olive oil and lemon.** No prep, just throw into a bowl and drizzle, adds freshness and colour.
+ **Pre-cut crudités and hummus.** Grab a pack of carrot/celery sticks and a hummus pot, done and delicious.
+ **Crisp wholegrain crackers.** Serve 4 or 5 on the side for extra texture and to scoop up every last bit of salad.

Cajun Prawn Alfredo Pasta

SERVES 4 **CALORIES: 546**

Spray oil
1 tbsp unsalted butter
300g raw king prawns, peeled and deveined
2 tsp Cajun seasoning
2 garlic cloves, grated
1 tsp dried oregano
500g fresh pasta (tagliatelle or linguine)
300ml hot chicken stock
150ml single cream
50g Parmesan, grated
Salt and black pepper, to taste
Chopped fresh parsley or chives, to serve

I wasn't in the mood to cook but wanted something that felt a bit indulgent... and this totally hit the spot. Creamy, spicy, cheesy and packed with prawns, it's the kind of dinner you'd happily eat on the sofa in your comfies with a glass of wine. Fresh pasta makes it that bit quicker, but it's all done in under 15 minutes anyway! My kind of cooking.

1. Spray a large pan with oil and add the butter, then place over a medium to high heat. Toss the prawns in the Cajun seasoning and cook for 2–3 minutes, until just pink. Remove and set aside.
2. Add the garlic and oregano to the pan and cook for 1 minute, until fragrant.
3. Add the fresh pasta and pour in the hot chicken stock. Simmer for 5–6 minutes, stirring gently, until the pasta is tender and most of the liquid has been absorbed.
4. Reduce the heat, add the single cream and Parmesan, and stir until the sauce is smooth and silky.
5. Put the prawns back into the pan, season to taste, and cook for another minute or two until everything's piping hot and coated in sauce.
6. Top with chopped parsley or chives, and serve.

SWAPS

→ Swap prawns for grilled chicken or leftover salmon. Still creamy, still full of flavour.
→ Swap single cream for light cream cheese. Slightly tangier, but still rich and smooth.
→ Swap Parmesan for pecorino. Saltier and just as delicious.

SIDES

+ Add garlic bread or flatbread. Ideal for mopping up all that creamy sauce.
+ Top with extra Parmesan and black pepper. The classic Alfredo finish.
+ Serve with a side of rocket or mixed greens. Adds a fresh contrast to the richness.

Gochujang and Cream Cheese Pasta

 SERVES 4   **CALORIES: 498**

Spray oil
2 tsp garlic purée
2 tsp ginger purée
1 tbsp gochujang (Korean chilli paste), to taste
1 tbsp tomato purée
300g dried pasta (penne and fusilli work well)
600ml hot vegetable stock
100g light cream cheese
1 tbsp honey
1 tsp soy sauce
Salt and black pepper, to taste

TO SERVE
1 spring onion, finely sliced
Sesame seeds or chilli flakes (optional)

SWAPS

→ **Swap cream cheese for mascarpone.** Extra indulgent and still silky smooth.
→ **Swap gochujang for chilli oil.** A different kind of heat, with a twist.
→ **Swap pasta for gnocchi.** Turns it into a proper comforting bowl.

I don't know who needs to hear this, but gochujang and cream cheese might just be the chaotic duo you didn't know your pasta needed. It sounds odd, I know, but trust me, it *works*. It's spicy, creamy, slightly sweet and dangerously addictive... even the kids went quiet while eating it, and that never happens. If you're in the mood for something a bit different but still quick and comforting, this is the one.

1. Spray a large pan with oil and place over a medium heat. Add the garlic purée and ginger purée and cook for 1–2 minutes, until fragrant.
2. Stir in the gochujang and tomato purée and cook for another minute, to bring out the flavour.
3. Add the pasta and pour in the hot stock. Simmer for 10–12 minutes, stirring often, until the pasta is tender and most of the liquid has reduced.
4. Lower the heat and stir in the cream cheese, honey and soy sauce. Mix until smooth and creamy. Season to taste.
5. Top with the spring onions, sprinkle with sesame seeds or chilli flakes, if you like, and serve.

SIDES

+ **Top with crispy onions or crushed peanuts.** Adds texture and crunch.
+ **Serve with roasted broccoli or pak choi.** Balances out the richness.
+ **Add shredded chicken or prawns.** For a protein boost and to make it more filling.

Creamy Sun-dried Tomato Tortellini

 SERVES 4 **CALORIES: 320**

Spray oil
1 small onion, finely diced
3 tsp garlic purée
1 tbsp tomato purée
1 tbsp sun-dried tomato paste
75g sun-dried tomatoes, roughly chopped
200ml hot vegetable stock
150ml single cream
500g fresh tortellini (cheese or spinach)
30g Parmesan, grated
Salt and black pepper, to taste
Fresh basil, to serve (optional)

This recipe came about after one of those chaotic days when I'd forgotten to defrost anything, had 15 minutes, and was absolutely starving. I grabbed a pack of tortellini, spotted an open jar of sun-dried tomatoes in the fridge, and just went with it. The result? Creamy, punchy, and weirdly feels like you've made way more effort than you actually have. It's now one of my go-tos when I need something quick that still tastes like a proper meal – no faff, barely any chopping and it always hits the spot.

1. Spray a large pan with oil and place over a medium heat. Add the onion and cook for 2–3 minutes, until soft. Stir in the garlic purée and cook for another minute.
2. Add the tomato purée and sun-dried tomato paste. Stir well, then mix in the chopped sun-dried tomatoes.
3. Pour in the hot stock and bring to a gentle simmer. Add the cream and stir through.
4. Tip in the tortellini and cook for 3–4 minutes, stirring gently, until the pasta is tender and the sauce has thickened.
5. Stir in the Parmesan, season to taste, and finish with fresh basil, if you fancy.

SWAPS

→ **Swap single cream for light crème fraîche.** Still creamy, but with a bit of a tang and fewer calories.
→ **Swap cheese tortellini for mushroom or butternut squash tortellini.** Adds a different flavour twist while keeping the same creamy base.
→ **Swap sun-dried tomato paste for roasted red pepper paste.** Still rich and vibrant but with a sweeter, milder finish.

SIDES

+ **Garlic and herb grilled chicken.** Season a couple of chicken breasts, pan-fry or air-fry, and slice over the top. Super easy and bulks out the meal.
+ **Pan-fried prawns with lemon.** Toss prawns in a pan with garlic, chilli flakes and a squeeze of lemon. They only take a few minutes and go beautifully with the creamy sauce.
+ **Toasted sourdough or crusty bread.** Pop a slice in the toaster and butter it. Done. Perfect for mopping up sauce.

Lemon, Garlic and Thyme Pasta

 SERVES 4 **CALORIES: 317**

Spray oil
1 small onion, finely diced
3 tsp garlic purée
Zest and juice of 1 lemon
1 tsp dried thyme (or a few sprigs of fresh, leaves stripped)
300ml hot vegetable stock
150ml single cream
500g fresh pasta (tagliatelle and linguine work well)
40g Parmesan, grated
Salt and black pepper, to taste
Extra lemon zest and chopped fresh parsley, to finish (optional)

SWAPS

- → **Swap single cream for light crème fraîche.** Adds a little tang and trims the calories without losing that creamy feel.
- → **Swap Parmesan for lighter Italian hard cheese.** Still gives that savoury, salty kick, just a little leaner.
- → **Add cooked chicken or prawns.** Stir in some shredded roast chicken or pan-fried prawns, for a boost of protein that works perfectly with the lemon and thyme.

This one just tastes like summer to me. It's fresh and lemony with a little hit of garlic and thyme, and it's the kind of pasta I'd happily eat outside with a glass of something cold and no shoes on. It's quick, simple and a nice change from the usual rich, cosy dinners I gravitate towards, still comforting, but with a bit of sunshine in every bite.

1. Spray a large pan with oil and place over a medium heat. Add the onion and cook for 2–3 minutes, until softened.
2. Stir in the garlic purée, lemon zest, lemon juice and thyme leaves. Cook for 1 minute, until fragrant.
3. Pour in the hot stock and the cream, then bring to a gentle simmer.
4. Add the fresh pasta and cook for 3–4 minutes, stirring gently to coat in the sauce.
5. Once the pasta is cooked and the sauce has thickened slightly, stir in the Parmesan. Season to taste and finish with a bit of lemon zest or chopped parsley, if you fancy.

SIDES

- + **Steamed green beans with a squeeze of lemon.** Bright, quick and pairs perfectly with the zesty flavours.
- + **Toasted sourdough with garlic butter.** Simple, but perfect for scooping up that creamy sauce.
- + **Rocket and shaved fennel salad.** Fresh, peppery and balances the creaminess of the pasta.

Pasta in a Pan

Rice & Easy

Marry Me Chicken Rice

❄ **GF**   **SERVES 4**   **CALORIES: 527**

Spray oil
500g chicken breast, diced
2 tbsp chicken seasoning
1 onion, finely diced
3 tsp garlic purée
2 tbsp sun-dried tomato paste
2 tsp dried oregano
1 tsp dried thyme
1 tsp dried parsley
1 tsp dried basil
300ml hot chicken stock
150ml single cream
500g cold cooked basmati rice (I use microwave rice)
80g cheese, grated (extra mature Cheddar, Red Leicester and full-fat mozzarella mix)
Salt and black pepper, to taste
Chilli flakes and chopped fresh parsley, to garnish (optional)

I made this a couple of years ago and it instantly became one of those recipes I couldn't stop making. It's packed with flavour, super creamy, a little bit cheesy, and the herby tomato sauce just works so well with the chicken and rice. I popped it on social media at the time and it got a great reaction, but honestly, it's just one of those dinners that speaks for itself. So simple, so delicious, and still one of my all-time faves.

1. Spray a large pan with oil and place over a medium to high heat. Add the diced chicken, sprinkle over the chicken seasoning and fry for 4–5 minutes, until browned.
2. Add the onion and cook for 2–3 minutes, until softened. Stir in the garlic purée and cook for 30 seconds.
3. Add the sun-dried tomato paste, herbs, hot stock and cream. Stir well and let it simmer for 2–3 minutes.
4. Stir through the cooked rice until everything's coated and heated through. Season to taste.
5. Top with the grated cheese and pop a lid on until it's melted.
6. Garnish with chilli flakes and chopped parsley if you fancy, then serve.

SWAPS

→ Swap chicken for diced reduced-fat halloumi. Pan-fry until golden first – salty, chewy and goes perfectly with the creamy, herby sauce.

→ Swap cream for light cream cheese. Still rich and smooth, with a little extra tang. Stir in with the stock until fully melted.

SIDES

+ **Garlicky wilted spinach.** Throw spinach into a hot pan with garlic and a splash of water – ready in 2 minutes and adds a bit of green.
+ **Crispy side salad.** Crunchy lettuce, cucumber, red onion, anything you've got in the fridge, with your favourite dressing.
+ **Mini garlic flatbreads.** Perfect for scooping, mopping and generally making sure no sauce gets left behind.

Hoisin Sticky Beef Fried Rice

❄ **GF** **SERVES 4** **CALORIES: 434**

Spray oil
500g lean 5% beef mince
1 onion, finely diced
2 mixed peppers, diced
3 tsp garlic purée
2 tsp ginger purée
3 tbsp hoisin sauce
1 tbsp dark soy sauce
1 tbsp light soy sauce
1 tbsp rice vinegar or white wine vinegar
500g cold cooked basmati rice (I use microwave rice)
1 tsp sesame oil (optional)
Salt and black pepper, to taste
Chopped spring onions and sesame seeds, to finish (optional)

When I'm craving a Chinese takeaway but don't fancy the price, the wait... or the food coma, this is what I make. It's sweet, sticky, a little bit spicy if you want it, and hits every single fakeaway craving without leaving the kitchen. No judgement if you eat it straight out of the pan. I've definitely done that.

1. Spray a large pan with oil and place over a medium to high heat. Add the beef mince and fry for 5 minutes, until browned, breaking it up as it cooks.
2. Add the onion and peppers and cook for 3–4 minutes until softened. Stir in the garlic purée and ginger purée and cook for another minute.
3. Add the hoisin, soy sauces and vinegar. Let it simmer for 1–2 minutes, until sticky and glossy.
4. Stir through the cooked rice until everything's coated and piping hot. Drizzle with sesame oil, if you like, and season to taste.
5. Top with spring onions and sesame seeds, if you like, and serve.

SWAPS

→ **Swap beef mince for Quorn mince.** A brilliant veggie alternative that cooks quickly and soaks up all that sticky hoisin flavour beautifully.
→ **Swap hoisin for teriyaki sauce.** Still sweet and sticky, but with a slightly different depth.
→ **Swap sesame oil for chilli oil.** Adds a kick of heat and extra flavour if you fancy a bit of spice.

SIDES

+ **Quick cucumber salad.** Thinly sliced cucumber tossed with rice vinegar, a pinch of sugar and sesame seeds; fresh, crunchy and ready in minutes.
+ **Stir-fried veggies.** Grab a bag of pre-chopped stir-fry veg and flash-fry it with a splash of soy sauce – simple, speedy and adds a good crunch.
+ **Mini veggie spring rolls (oven or air fryer).** Crispy, golden and perfect for dunking, ideal if you're going for full fakeaway vibes.

Satay Chicken Rice

❄ **GF** **SERVES 4** **CALORIES: 470**

Spray oil
500g chicken breast, diced
1 onion, finely diced
2 mixed peppers, diced
3 tsp garlic purée
2 tbsp Thai red curry paste
2 tbsp smooth peanut butter
1 tbsp soy sauce
1 tbsp honey
200ml hot chicken stock
120ml light coconut milk
500g cold cooked basmati rice (I use microwave rice)
Juice of ½ a lime
Salt and black pepper, to taste
Chopped fresh coriander and peanuts, to garnish (optional)

Some nights just need a big bowl of something saucy, nutty and satisfying, and this is exactly that. It's got those proper Thai fakeaway flavours but it's all done at home and without any drama. A bit of peanut butter, a spoonful of curry paste, and suddenly you've got something that tastes way fancier than you'd expect from the little effort involved. The kind of dinner that makes you feel like you've got your life together... even if you're still in your pyjamas at 5pm.

1. Spray a large pan with oil and place over a medium to high heat. Add the chicken and cook for 4–5 minutes, until browned all over.
2. Add the onion and peppers, cook for 2–3 minutes until soft, then stir in the garlic purée and cook for 30 seconds.
3. Stir through the Thai red curry paste and peanut butter until melted and fragrant. Add the soy sauce, honey, hot stock and coconut milk.
4. Simmer for 2–3 minutes, then stir in the cooked rice. Squeeze over the lime juice and season to taste.
5. Garnish with chopped coriander and peanuts, if you fancy, then serve.

SWAPS

→ **Swap chicken for prawns.** Quick to cook and they work beautifully with the Thai flavours – just toss them in for the final 5 minutes.

→ **Swap peanut butter for almond butter.** Still creamy and nutty, but a slightly milder taste and can be easier to digest.

→ **Swap coconut milk for light cream cheese.** Add at the end for a creamy twist if you're out of coconut milk – it still gives a lovely richness.

SIDES

+ **Mini prawn crackers.** Crispy, salty and perfect for scooping, brings those classic takeaway vibes without the faff.
+ **Chilli soy greens.** Quick-fry some green beans or tenderstem broccoli with a splash of soy sauce and chilli flakes for crunch and a bit of heat.
+ **Pickled carrot and cucumber slaw.** Slice thinly, splash with rice wine vinegar and sugar and leave for 10 minutes – fresh, zingy and cuts through the richness perfectly.

Garlic, Chilli and Ginger Prawn Rice

❄ GF **SERVES 4** **CALORIES: 330**

Spray oil
400g raw king prawns, peeled and deveined
1 onion, finely diced
150g tenderstem broccoli, chopped into bite-size pieces
6 tsp garlic purée
4 tsp ginger purée
1 red chilli, finely chopped (use half if you like it milder)
2 tbsp soy sauce
1 tbsp sweet chilli sauce
Juice of 1 lime
500g cold cooked basmati or jasmine rice (I use microwave rice)
Chilli oil, to drizzle (optional)
Chopped fresh coriander, to finish (optional)

Garlic, chilli and ginger prawns are one of my all-time favourites – I could honestly eat them on repeat. So I figured, why not turn them into a proper, full-on meal? This dish has all the bold flavours I love, but with rice, broccoli and loads of saucy goodness to make it feel a bit more satisfying. It's quick, easy, and totally hits the spot when I want something that feels a little bit special without the fuss.

1. Spray a large pan with oil and place over a medium to high heat. Add the prawns and cook for 2–3 minutes, until pink and just cooked, then set aside.
2. Add the onion and broccoli to the pan and cook for 3–4 minutes, until starting to soften. Add a splash of water and a lid if needed to help the broccoli steam.
3. Stir in the garlic purée, ginger purée and chilli and cook for another minute, until super fragrant.
4. Add the soy sauce, sweet chilli sauce and lime juice, then stir through the rice until piping hot and well coated.
5. Return the prawns to the pan, toss everything together and cook for 1 more minute.
6. Drizzle with chilli oil and sprinkle with chopped coriander, if you fancy.

SWAPS

→ **Swap prawns for tofu.** Crispy pan-fried tofu works brilliantly with the garlic, chilli and ginger flavours – just press and cube it, then fry until golden.
→ **Swap rice for wholegrain or cauliflower rice.** Wholegrain adds fibre, cauliflower rice lowers the carbs, both soak up the flavours beautifully.

SIDES

+ **Garlic soy mushrooms.** Pan-fry sliced mushrooms with a splash of soy sauce and a little garlic for a savoury, juicy side that's ready in minutes.
+ **Chilli-salt green beans.** Toss green beans in a hot pan with a sprinkle of salt and chilli flakes – crisp, spicy, and so moreish.
+ **Pickled carrot ribbons.** Quick-pickle carrot strips in a mix of vinegar and sugar, for a zingy crunch that cuts through the richness of the dish.

Chicken, Bacon and Tomato Rice

❄ GF · SERVES 4 · CALORIES: 570

Spray oil
500g chicken breast, diced
1 tsp smoked paprika
1 onion, finely diced
8 rashers of smoked bacon, chopped
4 tsp garlic purée or 4 garlic cloves, finely grated
1 tbsp tomato purée
1 x 400g tin of chopped tomatoes
1 tsp dried oregano
½ tsp chilli flakes (optional)
250ml hot chicken stock
500g cold cooked basmati rice (I use microwave rice)
Salt and black pepper, to taste
120g cheese, grated (I use extra mature Cheddar and Red Leicester)
Chopped fresh parsley, to garnish (optional)

You know those nights when it's cold, you're starving, and you want something proper tasty but still quick? That's exactly how this one came about. The smoky bacon, garlicky tomato sauce and cheesy golden top just hit the spot. It's the kind of meal that fills the kitchen with the best smells and has everyone asking what's for dinner before it's even finished. One pan, loads of flavour, no fuss and exactly what I need midweek.

1. Spray a large non-stick pan with oil and place over a medium to high heat. Add the chicken and paprika and fry for 4–5 minutes, until starting to brown.
2. Add the onion and bacon and cook for another 2–3 minutes, until softened and golden.
3. Stir in the garlic purée and tomato purée and cook for 1 minute to bring out the flavour. Add the chopped tomatoes, oregano, chilli flakes (if using) and hot chicken stock, and simmer for 2–3 minutes.
4. Stir in the cooked rice and mix well until everything is combined and piping hot. Season to taste.
5. Top with the grated cheese, then pop a lid on for 1–2 minutes, until melted.
6. Garnish with chopped parsley, if you like, and serve.

SWAPS

→ **Swap bacon for chorizo.** Adds a smoky, spicy kick – just 50g will totally change the flavour in the best way.

→ **Swap Cheddar and Red Leicester for full-fat mozzarella.** Gives that perfect stringy melt, still indulgent but a little lighter on flavour.

SIDES

+ **Steamed tenderstem broccoli.** Quick, green and adds a bit of crunch, balances the richness.
+ **Garlic flatbreads.** Perfect for scooping up every last bit of that cheesy tomato rice.
+ **Simple rocket salad.** Peppery, fresh and no cooking needed, a great contrast to the warm, cheesy rice.

Sausage and 'Nduja Rice

GF · **SERVES 4** · **CALORIES: 486**

This one's all about big flavour with minimal faff. The smoky sausage, spicy 'nduja and rich tomatoey rice hit just the right level of cosy and punchy. I made it once with what was knocking about in the fridge and now it's become a bit of a regular, especially when we want something warming but not too heavy. It's got that satisfying 'spoon straight from the pan' energy, and I'm not even sorry about it.

Spray oil
6 gluten-free pork sausages, cut into chunks (about 400g)
1 onion, finely diced
1 pepper (any colour), finely diced
3 tsp garlic purée
1 tbsp tomato purée
1 tbsp 'nduja paste
1 tsp smoked paprika
300ml hot chicken stock
500g cold cooked basmati rice (I use microwave rice)
Salt and black pepper, to taste
Chopped fresh parsley or chilli flakes, to garnish (optional)

1. Spray a large pan with oil and place over a medium to high heat. Add the sausage chunks and cook for 5–6 minutes, until browned and starting to crisp.
2. Add the onion and pepper and cook for another 3–4 minutes, until softened.
3. Stir in the garlic purée, tomato purée, 'nduja paste and paprika. Cook for 1–2 minutes until it smells amazing and everything's coated.
4. Pour in the hot chicken stock and bring to a simmer. Add the cooked rice, breaking it up with your spoon and mixing well until everything is hot and coated in the sauce.
5. Season to taste, garnish with chopped parsley or chilli flakes, if you fancy, and serve.

SWAPS

→ **Swap sausages for chicken sausages.** Still full of flavour, but a leaner option that lowers the calories without losing the comfort factor.

→ **Swap rice for cauliflower rice.** A lighter, lower-carb base that still soaks up the spicy, smoky sauce beautifully.

→ **Swap 'nduja for chorizo.** If you can't find 'nduja, diced chorizo works a treat – just fry it with the sausages for that same rich, smoky flavour.

SIDES

+ **Warm crusty bread.** Ideal for mopping up every last bit of that spicy, saucy rice, no fancy plating required.
+ **A crisp side salad.** Just mixed leaves, cucumber and whatever else is in the fridge, tossed in a quick vinaigrette – adds freshness and crunch.
+ **Steamed tenderstem broccoli.** Cooks in minutes and gives a bit of bite and colour, a great way to sneak some green onto the plate.

Cheesy Mexican-style Rice

❄ **GF** **SERVES 4** **CALORIES: 601**

Spray oil
100g chorizo, diced
500g chicken breast, diced
1 tbsp Mexican seasoning
1 onion, finely diced
2 mixed peppers, finely diced
4 tsp garlic purée or 4 garlic cloves, grated
1 tbsp tomato purée
120ml single cream
300ml hot chicken stock
500g cold cooked basmati rice (I use microwave rice)
120g cheese, grated (extra mature Cheddar, Red Leicester and full-fat mozzarella mix)
Salt and black pepper, to taste
Chilli flakes and chopped fresh coriander, to garnish (optional)

This one's been with me for years – it started as a quick midweek throw-together trying to recreate something my friend had made, and has slowly turned into one of those go-to dinners I just keep coming back to. I've tweaked it along the way (more cheese, always more cheese), and now it's exactly how we love it. Smoky, creamy, a little bit spicy and seriously satisfying. It's like a familiar favourite, but with a glow-up.

1. Spray a large non-stick pan with oil and place over a medium to high heat. Add the chorizo and cook for 1–2 minutes, until it starts to crisp and release its oils. Scoop out half and set aside for garnish.
2. Add the diced chicken to the pan along with the Mexican seasoning. Fry over a medium to high heat for 4–5 minutes, until browned all over.
3. Stir in the onion and peppers and continue to cook over a medium heat for another 2–3 minutes, until softened. Add the garlic purée and tomato purée and cook for 1 minute to take the raw edge off the tomato.
4. Pour in the cream and the hot chicken stock, then reduce to a medium heat and let it bubble gently for 1–2 minutes.
5. Stir in the cooked rice, mixing well until everything's hot and coated in the sauce. Season to taste. Sprinkle over the cheese, then turn off the heat and pop a lid on for 2–3 minutes until the cheese has melted.
6. Top with the crispy chorizo you set aside earlier and finish with chilli flakes and chopped coriander, if you like.

SWAPS

→ **Swap ready-made Mexican seasoning for individual spices.** Use 1 tsp smoked paprika, 1 tsp ground cumin, ½ tsp oregano, ½ tsp garlic granules and a pinch of chilli powder. Gives the same smoky depth with a little extra control over the heat.

→ **Swap chicken for Quorn pieces and use vegetable stock to make it veggie.** Still packed with protein and cooks quickly from frozen, ideal for a meat-free night.

SIDES

+ **Warm crusty bread.** To mop up all that cheesy, spicy sauce – no judgement if you use it like a spoon.
+ **Guac, salsa, sour cream and corn tortilla crisps.** A fun, build-your-own side that adds crunch, freshness and creaminess, perfect for piling high or scooping straight from the bowl.
+ **Charred corn on the cob.** Smoky, sweet and so easy, just a little butter and seasoning takes it to the next level.

Smoked Cajun Sausage Rice Salad

GF **SERVES 4** **CALORIES: 516**

2 tbsp light soy sauce
1 tbsp honey
3 tsp garlic purée
1 tbsp Cajun seasoning
Juice of 1 lime
500g cold cooked basmati rice (I use microwave rice)
Spray oil
240g cooked smoked sausage, chopped
1 red pepper, diced
1 small cucumber, diced
½ a small red onion, finely diced
A small handful of fresh coriander or parsley, chopped (optional)

FOR THE CREAMY CAJUN DRESSING
3 tbsp light mayo
3 tbsp 0% Greek yoghurt
1 tbsp honey
1 tsp Cajun seasoning
½ tsp garlic granules
Juice of ½ a lime

I've been obsessed with crispy rice salads lately, and this one hits every craving. Smoky sausage, crunchy fresh veg, a cheeky Cajun kick and that creamy, cooling drizzle to finish it all off. It's bold, it's full of texture and it's the kind of dish that somehow tastes even better cold straight from the fridge (spoon in hand, standing at the counter... you know the vibe).

1. In a bowl, mix together the soy sauce, honey, garlic purée, Cajun seasoning and lime juice. Add this to the cold rice and stir to coat evenly.
2. Spray a large non-stick pan with oil and place over a medium to high heat. Add the coated rice and press it down lightly. Let it cook undisturbed for 2–3 minutes, to crisp up underneath, then stir and repeat until you've got plenty of golden, crispy bits.
3. Take the rice off the heat and spread it out on a tray, then leave to cool.
4. In a large bowl, mix the smoked sausage, red pepper, cucumber, red onion and herbs, if using. Stir in the crispy rice.
5. Whisk together all the dressing ingredients. Drizzle over the salad and toss gently to coat. Pop it into the fridge if you've got time to chill it, or serve straight away.

SWAPS

→ **Swap smoked sausage for crispy tofu or reduced-fat halloumi.** Keeps that satisfying texture and smoky edge in a veggie-friendly version.
→ **Swap basmati rice for microwave brown rice.** Adds a boost of fibre and still crisps up beautifully in the pan.

SIDES

+ **Sliced avocado and chilli flakes.** Creamy, fresh, and a perfect balance for the spicy, smoky rice.
+ **Corn tortilla chips and fresh salsa.** Adds crunch and turns it into the ultimate sharing starter.
+ **Chilled mango salsa.** Sweet and juicy, a flavour contrast that elevates every mouthful.

Sticky Gochujang Pork Rice

❄ GF SERVES 4 CALORIES: 425

Spray oil
500g lean 5% pork mince
1 onion, finely diced
3 tsp garlic purée
1 tsp ginger purée
3 tbsp dark soy sauce
2 tbsp gochujang (Korean chilli paste)
1 tbsp honey
1 tbsp rice vinegar or lime juice
2 tbsp tomato ketchup
500g cold cooked basmati rice (I use microwave rice)
1 tsp sesame oil (optional)
Sliced spring onions and sesame seeds, to garnish

I'm always on the lookout for dinners that feel a bit different but don't take a mountain of effort, and this one ticks all the boxes. That sticky, spicy-sweet pork with fluffy rice and a bit of crunch on top of the spring onions… honestly, it's giving fakeaway, fridge raid, and midweek hero all in one. Plus, anything with gochujang is an instant yes from me.

1. Spray a large pan with oil and place over a medium to high heat. Add the pork mince and cook for 3–4 minutes, breaking it up as it cooks.
2. Once browned, stir in the onion and cook for 2–3 minutes, until softened. Add the garlic purée and ginger purée and fry for another minute.
3. In a small bowl, mix together the soy sauce, gochujang, honey, vinegar or lime juice and ketchup. Pour it into the pan and stir well, then cook for 2–3 minutes, until the pork has become sticky.
4. Add the cooked rice and stir everything together until fully coated. Drizzle over a little sesame oil, if using.
5. Top with sliced spring onions and sesame seeds, and serve!

SWAPS

→ **Swap pork mince for chicken or beef mince.** Still juicy and full of flavour, with a Korean-style twist.
→ **Swap gochujang for sriracha.** Not quite the same depth, but still brings a spicy-sweet kick.
→ **Swap cooked rice for cooked noodles.** Turns it into a sticky noodle bowl with just as much flavour.

SIDES

+ **Crispy fried egg.** Pop one on top – the yolk mixes beautifully with the sticky rice.
+ **Steamed tenderstem broccoli.** Adds crunch and colour with very little effort.
+ **Pickled cucumber or radish.** A sharp, fresh contrast to the rich, sticky pork.

Creamy Garlic and Parmesan Rice

❄ GF SERVES 4 CALORIES: 318

Spray oil
1 onion, finely diced
6 tsp garlic purée
500g cold cooked basmati rice (I use microwave rice)
150ml single cream
300ml hot chicken or vegetable stock
60g Parmesan, grated
Salt and black pepper, to taste
Chopped fresh parsley, to garnish (optional)

If there's one thing I'll never get bored with, it's garlic and Parmesan. This rice is creamy, cheesy and packed with flavour, one of those throw-together dinners that feels like way more effort than it actually is. I usually serve it up with whatever protein I've got in, and some quick veg on the side to make it a proper meal. It's comforting, versatile and always a winner in our house.

1. Spray a large pan with oil and place over a medium heat. Add the onion and cook for 3–4 minutes until softened, then stir in the garlic purée and cook for another minute.
2. Add the cooked rice, breaking it up with a spoon, followed by the cream and the hot stock. Stir until the rice is fully coated and everything is warmed through.
3. Mix in the Parmesan until melted and creamy. Season well with salt and black pepper to taste and top with a bit of chopped parsley, if you fancy.

SWAPS

→ **Swap cream for light cream cheese.** Gives a rich, velvety texture with a subtle tang, a great lower-calorie option that still feels indulgent.
→ **Swap white rice for wholegrain or microwave quinoa.** Adds extra fibre and a nuttier flavour, a simple switch that still soaks up the creamy sauce beautifully.
→ **Swap onion for leek.** A softer, sweeter flavour that melts down into the sauce and gives it a lovely mellow base.

SIDES

+ **Garlic and herb chicken strips.** Pan-fry thinly sliced chicken breast with garlic granules, mixed herbs and a squeeze of lemon – juicy, simple and a perfect match for the creamy rice.
+ **Crispy halloumi bites.** Cube reduced-fat halloumi and fry until golden on all sides – the salty crunch cuts through the creaminess and gives it serious cosy vibes.
+ **Seared steak slices.** Quickly pan-fry thin steak strips with salt, black pepper and a touch of mustard, then slice and serve on the rice for a proper treat that still feels easy.

Lemon and Oregano Rice

❄ GF SERVES 4 CALORIES: 382

Spray oil
1 small onion, finely diced
4 tsp garlic purée
250g uncooked basmati rice
600ml hot vegetable stock
Zest and juice of 1 lemon
1 tbsp dried oregano
1 tsp dried parsley
Salt and black pepper, to taste

TO GARNISH
Crumbled feta
Chopped fresh parsley
Lemon wedges

This rice is light, zesty and full of flavour, the kind of dish that goes with everything but still holds its own. The lemon and oregano give it that classic Greek flavour, and the feta on top adds the perfect salty finish. It's fresh, simple and ideal as a side or even on its own with a big spoon of tzatziki.

1. Spray a large pan with oil and place over a medium heat. Add the onion and cook for 2–3 minutes, until softened. Stir in the garlic purée and cook for another 30 seconds.
2. Add the rice, hot stock, lemon zest and juice, oregano and dried parsley. Stir well and bring to the boil.
3. Turn the heat down low and cook with a lid on for 10–12 minutes, stirring occasionally, until the rice is tender and most of the liquid has been absorbed.
4. Season to taste with salt and black pepper. Fluff the rice with a fork, garnish with crumbled feta, fresh parsley and lemon wedges, and serve.

SWAPS

→ **Swap basmati for long-grain or jasmine rice.** Just as fluffy, with a slightly different texture.
→ **Swap dried parsley for fresh mint or dill.** Adds a more traditional Greek flavour.
→ **Swap vegetable stock for chicken stock.** A bit richer, if you're not keeping it veggie.

SIDES

+ Serve with grilled chicken, reduced-fat halloumi or lamb koftas. Turns it into a full, satisfying meal.
+ Add a dollop of tzatziki or 0% Greek yoghurt. Creamy, tangy and refreshing.
+ Top with olives or a spoon of tapenade. For a briny, salty contrast.

Rice & Easy

Smoky Chicken and Pineapple Rice

❄ GF SERVES 4 CALORIES: 498

Spray oil
400g diced chicken breast
1 tsp garlic purée
1 tsp ginger purée
1 tsp all-purpose seasoning
1 tsp ground allspice
1 tsp smoked paprika
1 tbsp honey
2 tbsp soy sauce
1 tbsp tomato purée
1 x 227g tin of pineapple chunks in juice, drained, juice reserved
1 red pepper, diced
500g cold cooked basmati rice (I use microwave rice)
Juice of ½ a lime
Chopped fresh coriander or spring onions, to serve

This one's bursting with flavour, sweet, smoky, a little bit spicy and so easy to throw together. Inspired by the Caribbean, the combo of juicy pineapple, spiced chicken and sticky rice just works... it's like a little holiday in a bowl. It's one of those meals that feels a bit different but is still totally family-friendly.

1. Spray a large pan with oil and place over a medium to high heat. Add the chicken and cook for 5–6 minutes, until starting to brown.
2. Stir in the garlic purée, ginger purée, all-purpose seasoning, allspice, paprika, honey, soy sauce, tomato purée and the juice from the pineapple tin. Mix well and simmer for 2–3 minutes.
3. Add the red pepper and pineapple chunks, then stir through the cooked rice. Mix until everything is coated and piping hot.
4. Squeeze over the lime juice, top with chopped coriander or spring onions, and serve.

SWAPS

→ **Swap chicken breast for boneless thighs.** Adds extra juiciness and flavour.
→ **Swap pineapple chunks for mango.** Brings the same sweet balance with a twist.
→ **Swap basmati rice for microwave jasmine or brown rice.** Whatever you've got in works!

SIDES

+ **Serve with fried plantain or corn on the cob.** Adds even more tropical flavour.
+ **Top with a spoonful of chilli jam or hot sauce.** If you like it fiery.
+ **Add a side of black beans or avocado.** Great for bulking it out and adding more texture.

Rice & Easy

Chorizo and Butterbean Rice

❄ GF SERVES 4 CALORIES: 491

This is one of those dinners that feels bold and comforting all at once. The smoky chorizo, creamy butterbeans and soft basmati rice all come together in one pan, and it's ready in no time. It's hearty, satisfying and packed with flavour, the kind of meal you'll end up making on repeat.

Spray oil
1 onion, finely diced
120g chorizo, diced
2 tsp garlic purée
1 tsp smoked paprika
½ tsp dried thyme
1 tbsp tomato purée
1 x 400g tin of butterbeans, drained and rinsed
100ml hot chicken stock
500g cold cooked basmati rice (I use microwave rice)
Salt and black pepper, to taste
Chopped fresh parsley or lemon wedges, to serve (optional)

1. Spray a large pan with oil and place over a medium heat. Add the onion and chorizo and cook for 2–3 minutes, until softened and the chorizo starts to crisp and release its oil. Stir in the garlic purée and cook for 30 seconds or so.
2. Add the paprika, thyme and tomato purée, and cook for 1 minute to coat everything in the flavours.
3. Tip in the butterbeans and pour in the hot stock. Simmer for 2–3 minutes, until the beans are warmed through and the liquid slightly reduces.
4. Stir in the cooked rice and mix well to coat. Cook for a further 2–3 minutes, until piping hot.
5. Season to taste, and finish with chopped parsley or a squeeze of lemon, if you like.

SWAPS

→ **Swap chorizo for smoked sausage or diced bacon.** Still smoky and full of flavour.
→ **Swap butterbeans for kidney beans or black beans.** Easy to adapt with what you have.
→ **Swap chicken stock for vegetable stock.** To make it flexi or meat-free (just sub the chorizo, too).

SIDES

+ **Serve with a crisp salad or slaw.** To balance out the richness.
+ **Top with garlic mayo or aïoli.** Creamy and delicious with the smoky chorizo.
+ **Add a few olives or roasted red peppers.** A little extra Mediterranean flair.

Rice & Easy

Wrap It Up

Chicken Tikka and Mango Flatbreads

SERVES 4   **CALORIES: 527**

This is a proper flavour bomb and one we go back to time and time again. That combo of spiced chicken, sticky mango chutney, fresh salsa and minty yoghurt is unreal, like a fakeaway and a summer BBQ had a baby. The kids love building their own, my husband piles his sky-high, and I'm just there making sure no one nicks the last bit of mango salsa!

Spray oil
500g chicken breast, diced
2 tbsp tikka curry paste
1 tsp garlic granules
Salt and black pepper, to taste
1 red onion, finely sliced
4 soft flatbreads or naan-style wraps
100g mango chutney
A small handful of fresh coriander, chopped (optional)

FOR THE FRESH MANGO SALSA
1 ripe mango, finely diced
½ a red pepper, finely diced
1 spring onion, finely sliced
Juice of ½ a lime
A small handful of fresh coriander, chopped (optional)

FOR THE MINTED YOGHURT
120g 0% Greek yoghurt
1 tbsp mint sauce
Juice of ½ a lemon

1. Spray a large non-stick pan with oil and place over a medium to high heat. Toss the chicken with the tikka paste, garlic granules and a pinch of salt and black pepper, then add to the pan. Fry for around 7–8 minutes, until golden and cooked through.
2. Push the chicken to one side of the pan and add the sliced onion. Cook for a couple of minutes, until softened and lightly charred.
3. While that's cooking, mix together your mango salsa ingredients in a small bowl, and set aside.
4. In a separate bowl, stir together the yoghurt, mint sauce, lemon juice and a pinch of salt, until smooth.
5. Warm your flatbreads in the microwave. To build, spread a little mango chutney over each flatbread, top with the tikka chicken and onions, and spoon over the mango salsa. Drizzle with the minted yoghurt and sprinkle with chopped coriander, if you fancy it.
6. Fold, wrap or just grab a napkin and get stuck in!

SWAPS

- → **Swap chicken for reduced-fat halloumi.** Adds a salty, creamy twist and keeps it veggie-friendly.
- → **Swap mango chutney for hot chilli jam.** Gives you a sweet-spicy lift instead of the mellow mango flavour.

SIDES

+ **Crispy onion bhajis (shop-bought).** Makes it feel like a proper fakeaway night.
+ **Cucumber raita.** Use leftover minted yoghurt and add diced cucumber, cooling and crisp.
+ **Spiced potato wedges.** Oven-roasted with tikka seasoning for added comfort food vibes.

Loaded Veg and Pepperoni Baguette Pizza

SERVES 4 **CALORIES: 419**

2 part-baked white baguettes
3 tbsp tomato purée
1 tsp garlic granules
1 tsp dried oregano
1 tbsp olive oil (optional)
Salt and black pepper, to taste
1 red onion, finely sliced
½ a red pepper, thinly sliced
½ a green pepper, thinly sliced
100g tinned sweetcorn, drained
80g sliced pepperoni
120g full-fat mozzarella, grated (or a mozzarella/extra mature Cheddar mix)

TO SERVE
Chopped fresh basil or parsley (optional)
Hot honey, to drizzle (optional)

This one takes me right back to being a teenager, throwing together makeshift pizzas on baguettes after school with whatever we could find in the fridge. Fast-forward a few years (okay, maybe more than a few) and I'm still doing it, just with a bit more cheese and slightly less chaos in the kitchen. It's one of those easy dinners that feels nostalgic but still hits the spot every time. Crispy, cheesy, a little bit messy – and always a winner with the kids, too!

1. Preheat your oven to 220°C/200°C (fan) and pop a large baking tray in to heat up.
2. Slice the baguettes in half lengthways and place them cut side up on a sheet of baking paper. Mix the tomato purée, garlic granules, oregano, olive oil (if using) and a pinch of salt and black pepper in a bowl. Spread it over each baguette.
3. Top with sliced red onion and peppers, sweetcorn and pepperoni. Scatter over the cheese and transfer the baguettes (still on the baking paper) straight onto the hot baking tray.
4. Bake for 10–12 minutes, until crisp at the edges and golden and melty on top.
5. Finish with a bit of chopped basil or parsley and a drizzle of hot honey, if you fancy it.

SWAPS

→ **Swap white baguette for wholegrain or multiseeded.** Adds fibre and a nuttier taste, still bakes crisp and delicious.
→ **Swap pepperoni for grilled chicken strips or lean bacon.** Cuts down on fat while keeping the meaty flavour.
→ **Swap mozzarella for extra mature Cheddar or Red Leicester.** Offers a different melt and flavour.

SIDES

+ **Garlic and herb potato wedges.** Roast some frozen wedges or baby potatoes tossed in garlic granules and dried herbs, for a no-fuss side that always hits the spot.
+ **Crispy side slaw.** Grab some pre-made coleslaw, or mix your own with shredded cabbage, carrot and a dollop of light mayo – crunchy, creamy and refreshing.
+ **Cucumber and tomato salad with balsamic drizzle.** Simple, light and fresh, cuts through the richness and adds colour to the plate with basically no effort.

Lazy BBQ Beef Enchiladas

SERVES 4 **CALORIES: 482**

Some days I want all the comfort of enchiladas... without the whole roll-and-bake situation. This is a great lazy version – everything gets chopped, stirred and chucked into one pan, even the wraps. No judgement, no faff, just cheesy BBQ beef goodness in 15 minutes. It's like midweek chaos wrapped in melted cheese, and honestly, what more do you need?

Spray oil
500g lean 5% beef mince
1 red onion, finely diced
2 peppers (any colour), sliced
3 tsp garlic purée
1 tbsp smoked paprika
1 tsp ground cumin
200g passata
4 tbsp BBQ sauce
100ml hot beef stock
4 soft tortilla wraps, sliced into strips
Salt and black pepper, to taste
120g cheese, grated (extra mature Cheddar, full-fat mozzarella and Red Leicester mix)
Chopped fresh coriander or parsley, to garnish (optional)

1. Spray a large pan with oil and place over a medium to high heat. Add the mince and let it brown for 4–5 minutes, breaking it up as it cooks.
2. Add the onion and peppers, cooking for another 3–4 minutes until softened.
3. Stir in the garlic purée, smoked paprika and cumin and cook for 30 seconds.
4. Pour in the passata, BBQ sauce and hot beef stock. Stir through the sliced tortilla strips and season to taste. Simmer for 2–3 minutes, until thickened slightly, then sprinkle over the cheese mix.
5. Pop a lid on (or cover with foil if needed) and let the cheese melt for 2 minutes.
6. Garnish with chopped herbs, if you like, and serve!

SWAPS

→ **Swap the beef mince for turkey mince.** A lighter option that still soaks up the smoky flavours.
→ **Use wholemeal wraps instead of white.** Adds extra fibre and a nuttier flavour.
→ **Switch BBQ sauce for chipotle salsa.** For a spicier, smokier kick with a little more depth.

SIDES

+ **Simple green salad with lime dressing.** Something fresh and zesty to balance the richness.
+ **Crispy corn tortilla chips + guac or salsa.** Adds crunch and a fun sharing vibe.
+ **Microwave sweetcorn with a squeeze of lime.** Quick, sweet and zingy, works perfectly with BBQ flavours.

Sweet Chilli Chicken and Bacon Wrap

SERVES 4   **CALORIES: 560**

Wraps like this are my go-to when I want something delicious but super quick and easy. The chicken and bacon go all sticky and caramelised with the sweet chilli sauce, and the Cheddar melts into everything perfectly once it's toasted. Add some crunch from the salad and cucumber and it's got that perfect mix of hot, cold, soft and crisp. It's one of those dinners that feels like a treat but doesn't make a mess of the kitchen, and that's definitely a win for me.

Spray oil
4 rashers of smoked bacon, chopped
500g chicken breast, sliced
2 tsp garlic granules
Salt and black pepper, to taste
6 tbsp sweet chilli sauce
4 medium tortilla wraps
4 tbsp light mayo
½ a head of shredded lettuce
1 red pepper, thinly sliced
½ a cucumber, thinly sliced
80g extra mature Cheddar, grated

1. Spray a large pan with oil and place over a medium to high heat. Fry the chopped bacon for 2 minutes, then add the chicken and garlic granules. Season and cook for 6–8 minutes, until golden and cooked through.
2. Stir in the sweet chilli sauce and coat everything well. Let it bubble for 1 minute, then turn off the heat.
3. Lay out your wraps and spread with 1 tablespoon of mayo each. Add the lettuce, red pepper, cucumber, the chicken and bacon mix and 20g of grated Cheddar per wrap.
4. Fold the wraps up tightly. Wipe out the pan if needed, then toast each wrap, seam side down, for 1–2 minutes per side, until golden and crisp.
5. Slice and serve.

SWAPS

→ **Swap chicken for sliced steak or crispy halloumi, omitting the bacon.** Great if you want a twist or a veggie option.
→ **Swap Cheddar for full-fat mozzarella or Red Leicester.** Try different melty vibes to suit your taste.
→ **Swap mayo for garlic yoghurt or sriracha mayo.** Adds creaminess or a spicy kick, depending on your mood.

SIDES

+ **Air fryer wedges or sweet potato fries.** Keep it feeling like a proper takeaway.
+ **Crispy corn ribs or grilled corn on the cob.** Something a bit different on the side.
+ **Light crunchy slaw.** Balances the richness and adds colour to the plate.

Lamb Pitta Pockets with Salad and Minted Yoghurt

SERVES 4 **CALORIES: 550**

500g 20% lamb mince
1 small red onion, finely diced
2 tsp garlic granules
1 tsp ground cumin
1 tsp ground coriander
1 tsp smoked paprika
1 tbsp fresh mint, finely chopped
Salt and black pepper, to taste
4 white pitta breads
1 tbsp olive oil (for brushing)
A bag of mixed salad leaves, to serve
½ a cucumber, thinly sliced, to serve

FOR THE MINTED YOGHURT SAUCE
4 tbsp 0% Greek yoghurt
Juice of ½ a lemon
1 tsp mint sauce

SWAPS

→ **Swap lamb mince for beef mince.** Slightly leaner but still flavourful and juicy.
→ **Swap Greek yoghurt for light sour cream or mayo.** A creamy twist if you're out of yoghurt.
→ **Swap white pitta for wholemeal pitta.** Adds fibre and keeps it feeling hearty.

This one's a proper treat and feels like something you'd get from a really good street food stall. The lamb is packed with flavour, smoky, herby, a little bit spicy, and it all gets sealed into a pitta and toasted in the pan until golden and crisp. That contrast with the cool, minty yoghurt and fresh salad is just perfect. It's one of those dinners that looks impressive but takes hardly any effort. My kind of fakeaway.

1. Put the lamb mince, red onion, garlic granules, cumin, coriander, paprika, chopped mint, salt and black pepper into a bowl. Mix everything together really well with your hands until fully combined.
2. Take each pitta and carefully slice it across the side edge (not the top), using a serrated knife to create a pocket, going about three-quarters of the way through.
3. Stuff each pitta evenly with the lamb mixture, pressing it in firmly so it holds together but not overfilling. Brush both sides of each stuffed pitta with a little olive oil. Cut each stuffed pitta in half, then heat a large pan over a medium heat.
4. Place the pittas cut-side down in the pan to crisp the lamb edges, then cook for 4–5 minutes on each side, gently pressing down with a spatula to seal the cut ends, crisp the bread and make sure the lamb cooks through. You may need to do this in batches, depending on pan size.
5. While they cook, stir together the yoghurt, lemon juice and mint sauce to make your quick minted yoghurt dip.
6. Serve the crisped pitta halves with salad leaves, cucumber slices, and a dollop of the minted yoghurt.

SIDES

+ **Spiced potato wedges.** Great for scooping up any sauce or filling.
+ **Grilled halloumi slices.** Adds saltiness and turns it into a bigger feast.
+ **Tomato and red onion salad.** Brings a fresh zing that balances the richness.

Burger Loaded Pittas

SERVES 4 **CALORIES: 395**

Spray oil
500g lean 5% beef mince
1 small onion, finely diced
4 white pitta breads
4 slices of American-style cheese
80g shredded iceberg lettuce
Salt and black pepper, to taste
Sesame seeds, to garnish (optional)

FOR THE BURGER SAUCE
4 tbsp light mayo
1 tbsp ketchup
1 tbsp American mustard
2 small gherkins, finely chopped
½ tsp onion granules
½ tsp garlic granules
½ tsp paprika
2 tsp pickle juice or white vinegar

This is one of those dinners that always goes down a storm in our house. It's got all the right vibes – salty beef, melty cheese, loads of lettuce and that classic burger sauce, but instead of faffing about with buns, I just load it all onto toasted pittas and call it a night. The kids love it, my husband loves it, and I love that it's all done in one pan with barely any mess. It's our kind of midweek fakeaway, quick, easy and everyone clears their plate.

1. Spray a large pan with oil and place over a medium to high heat. Add the beef mince and onion and cook together for 6–8 minutes, breaking the meat down finely, until browned and cooked through. Season well with salt and black pepper.
2. Meanwhile, stir together all the burger sauce ingredients in a small bowl.
3. Toast the pittas whole in the toaster for 30–60 seconds, just until warm and slightly puffed.
4. Lay the pittas flat on plates or a board. Add a slice of American cheese on top of each one, then spoon over the hot beef mixture so the cheese melts slightly underneath.
5. Top with shredded lettuce and a big drizzle of your homemade burger sauce and garnish with sesame seeds (if using). Serve immediately.

SWAPS

- → **Swap beef mince for turkey or chicken mince.** Still juicy, but a little leaner.
- → **Swap American cheese slices for grated extra mature Cheddar or full-fat mozzarella.** Melts just as well, with a twist on the flavour.
- → **Swap white pittas for wholemeal or folded flatbreads.** Adds fibre and makes it feel even more like a wrap-pizza hybrid.

SIDES

- + **Skin-on fries with burger seasoning.** Adds crunch and that classic takeaway feel.
- + **Loaded sweetcorn salad with lime and coriander.** Fresh, zingy and balances the richness of the beef.
- + **Onion rings.** Crispy, golden and perfect for dunking in leftover burger sauce.

Quick Sloppy Joe Toasties

SERVES 4 **CALORIES: 500**

This dinner came about on one of those nights – I had mince in the fridge, bread in the cupboard and about 15 minutes to feed everyone before the meltdown hour kicked in. So I threw together this sloppy, cheesy toastie situation and honestly... it was a stroke of genius. The beef's got that sweet, smoky flavour, the slaw brings the crunch, and once it's all melted together in a golden toastie? Game over. The kids wolfed it down without a single complaint, and I got that look of approval from both Harry and Lottie that says, 'You've smashed it.'

Spray oil
500g lean 5% beef mince
1 small onion, finely diced
1 tbsp tomato purée
250ml passata
4 tbsp ketchup
2 tsp Worcestershire sauce
1 tsp smoked paprika
Salt and black pepper, to taste

FOR THE SLAW (USE SHOP-BOUGHT IF YOU PREFER)
100g white cabbage, finely shredded
1 small carrot, grated
¼ a red onion, very finely sliced
2 tbsp light mayo
1 tsp white vinegar

FOR THE TOASTIES
8 slices of soft white bread
100g extra mature Cheddar, grated
Spray oil or unsalted butter (for toasting)

1. Spray a large pan with oil and place over a medium to high heat. Add the beef mince and onion and cook for 6–8 minutes, until the meat is browned and broken down. Season with salt and black pepper.
2. Stir in the tomato purée, passata, ketchup, Worcestershire sauce and paprika. Simmer for 2–3 minutes, until rich and saucy.
3. While that simmers, mix together the cabbage, carrot, red onion, mayo, vinegar and seasoning to make your quick slaw.
4. Lay out the bread slices. Top half of them with a spoonful of saucy beef, a layer of slaw and a handful of grated Cheddar. Add the top slices and press down gently.
5. Wipe out the pan, if needed, then return to a medium heat. Spray or butter both sides of each sandwich, then toast for 2–3 minutes per side until golden and crisp, and the cheese has melted.
6. Slice and serve hot.

SWAPS

→ **Swap beef mince for Quorn or turkey mince.** Lighter but still flavour-packed and saucy.
→ **Swap Cheddar for Red Leicester or burger cheese slices.** Switch up the flavour while keeping that melt.
→ **Swap white bread for brioche or sourdough.** A bakery-style twist that toasts beautifully.

SIDES

+ **Frozen oven chips.** Minimal prep, maximum crisp, keeps the fakeaway vibes going.
+ **Mixed bagged salad with a honey mustard drizzle.** No chopping needed, adds freshness and zing to every bite.

Chicken Caesar Folded Wraps

SERVES 4 **CALORIES: 460**

Spray oil
500g chicken breast, thinly sliced
1 tsp garlic granules
1 tsp smoked paprika
Salt and black pepper, to taste
4 bacon medallions (optional, but adds a lovely flavour)
4 large tortilla wraps
60g grated Parmesan
100g shredded romaine or iceberg lettuce

FOR THE CAESAR SAUCE
4 tbsp light mayo
1 tsp Dijon mustard
1 tsp lemon juice
1 tbsp grated Parmesan
1 small garlic clove, finely grated
½ tsp Worcestershire sauce

Some dinners just hit the spot, and this is one of them. It's got all the best bits of a Caesar salad, but folded, toasted and taken to a whole new level. The garlicky chicken, the quick homemade Caesar sauce, the melty cheese... It feels like something you'd order from a café, but it's dead easy and the kids absolutely love it. Honestly, I could eat this one on repeat.

1. Spray a large pan with oil and place over a medium to high heat. Season the chicken with garlic granules, paprika, salt and black pepper. Add to the pan and cook for 5–7 minutes, until golden and cooked through. Remove and set aside.
2. If using bacon, add the medallions to the same pan and cook for 2–3 minutes each side, until crisp. Chop or tear into pieces.
3. While the chicken cooks, whisk together all the Caesar sauce ingredients with a pinch each of salt and pepper in a bowl.
4. For each wrap, make a single cut from the centre out to the bottom edge to help with folding. Imagine the wrap in quarters, starting with the bottom left corner and working clockwise.
   - Spread a little Caesar sauce on the first quarter.
   - Add the chicken to the next.
   - Sprinkle bacon, if using, and Parmesan on the third.
   - Add lettuce with more sauce to the final quarter.
5. Fold the wrap up clockwise, one quarter at a time, into a triangle shape.
6. Lightly spray the pan with oil and cook the wraps over a medium heat for 2–3 minutes per side, until golden and crisp and the cheese is melty.
7. Serve hot, with extra Caesar sauce for dipping!

SWAPS

→ **Swap chicken breast for rôtisserie chicken.** Saves even more time.
→ **Swap Parmesan for grated extra mature Cheddar.** Still cheesy, with a slightly different bite.
→ **Swap tortilla wraps for wholemeal.** Adds fibre and a more rustic flavour.

SIDES

+ **Ready-to-eat coleslaw.** Crunchy and cool alongside the warm wrap.
+ **Baby cucumbers and cherry tomatoes.** Fresh, sweet and great for dipping in leftover sauce.
+ **Crisps or tortilla chips.** Adds a salty crunch to keep things fun and casual.

Korean BBQ Beef and Kimchi Slaw Pittas

SERVES 4 **CALORIES: 486**

1 tbsp oil
500g lean 5% beef mince
1 small onion, finely sliced
1 tbsp garlic and ginger purée
3 tbsp light soy sauce
2 tbsp dark soy sauce
2 tbsp Korean BBQ sauce
1 tbsp honey
1 tsp rice vinegar
Salt and black pepper, to taste

FOR THE KIMCHI SLAW
150g pre-shredded coleslaw mix
2 tbsp light mayo
2 tbsp kimchi, chopped
1 tsp sesame seeds
Juice of ½ a lime

TO SERVE
4 white pitta breads, toasted or warmed
Sliced spring onions and chopped fresh coriander (optional)

These pittas are full of flavour and so quick to pull together, perfect for busy evenings when you want something a bit different. The sticky Korean-style beef and crunchy kimchi slaw make such a good combo – sweet, smoky, tangy and a little bit spicy. An easy dinner with loads of flavour in every bite.

1. Heat the oil in a large pan over a medium to high heat. Add the mince and onion and cook for 5–6 minutes until browned.
2. Stir in the garlic and ginger purée, both soy sauces, the Korean BBQ sauce, honey, rice vinegar and a splash of water.
3. Let it bubble for 3–4 minutes until glossy and slightly sticky. Season to taste.
4. Meanwhile, combine the coleslaw mix with the mayo, chopped kimchi, sesame seeds and lime juice to make the slaw.
5. Toast the pittas and slice them open.
6. Stuff each one with a generous spoon of the Korean beef and a heap of kimchi slaw.
7. Top with sliced spring onions and chopped coriander (if using).

SWAPS

→ **Swap beef mince for chicken or turkey mince.** A lighter twist with the same saucy flavour.
→ **Swap kimchi for chilli jam in the slaw.** Adds sweetness and a different kind of kick.
→ **Swap pittas for flatbreads.** Great for folding and loading up like tacos.

SIDES

+ **Serve with air-fried edamame.** A crunchy, salty side that goes perfectly.
+ **Add sriracha or a hot sauce drizzle.** For extra heat and depth.
+ **Pair with sesame cucumber ribbons.** A fresh, cooling contrast to the spice.

Butter Chicken Loaded Naan

SERVES 4 **CALORIES: 487**

Spray oil
500g chicken breast, diced
1 tbsp tandoori curry powder
3 tsp garlic purée
3 tsp ginger purée
2 tbsp tomato purée
1 tbsp curry paste
200ml passata
100ml light single cream
1 tbsp unsalted butter
Salt and black pepper, to taste
4 plain naan breads (shop-bought)

TO SERVE
2 tbsp 0% Greek yoghurt
Fresh coriander
Red chilli slices or mango chutney (optional)

If your family loves a fakeaway night as much as mine, these loaded naans are a winner. The butter chicken is rich, creamy and mildly spiced, perfect for all ages, and it's piled onto soft, warm naan breads with your favourite toppings.

1. Spray a large pan with oil and place over a medium to high heat. Add the chicken and curry powder and cook for 3–4 minutes, until sealed.
2. Stir in the garlic, ginger and tomato purées and curry paste and cook for 1 minute.
3. Pour in the passata and cream, then add the butter. Simmer for 5–6 minutes, until thickened and the chicken is fully cooked. Season to taste.
4. Meanwhile, warm the naan breads in the toaster or microwave until soft and heated through.
5. Once everything's ready, load up each naan with a generous spoonful of the cheesy butter chicken.
6. Top with a dollop of Greek yoghurt, fresh coriander and some chillies or mango chutney, if you like.

SWAPS

→ **Swap chicken for tinned chickpeas or paneer.** A quick, protein-packed veggie alternative.
→ **Swap cream for light coconut milk.** Adds a subtle sweetness and makes it dairy-free.
→ **Swap naan for folded flatbreads.** Easier to hold and perfect for loading up.

SIDES

+ **Serve with cucumber raita.** A cool, refreshing contrast to the creamy spice.
+ **Add crispy onions on top.** Crunchy and packed with savoury flavour.
+ **Pair with a chopped salad.** Adds freshness and colour to the plate.

Chicken, Halloumi and Pesto Folded Wrap

SERVES 4 **CALORIES: 541**

Spray oil
400g chicken breast, thinly sliced
1 tbsp garlic granules
Salt and black pepper, to taste
150g reduced-fat halloumi, sliced
4 tortilla wraps
4 tbsp light cream cheese
4 tsp green pesto
A handful of rocket (optional)

FOR THE CREAMY RED PESTO SAUCE (ENOUGH FOR ALL 4 WRAPS)
2 tbsp red pesto
2 tbsp light mayo
2 tbsp 0% Greek yoghurt
Juice of ½ lemon

SWAPS

→ Swap halloumi for full-fat mozzarella slices. Melty and satisfying, but slightly lighter and milder.
→ Swap chicken for grilled mushrooms or courgette strips. A delicious veggie option that still gives you bite.
→ Swap red pesto sauce for a sriracha mayo drizzle. A spicy twist if you're after something with more kick.

SIDES

+ **Crispy sweet potato wedges.** Roasted with paprika for a hearty side that keeps the wrap the star.
+ **Simple cucumber and tomato salad.** Fresh, crunchy and takes 2 minutes to throw together.
+ **A handful of tortilla chips with hummus or guac.** Great for scooping up extra sauce or finishing off any leftover fillings.

I threw this together on a day when I wanted something tasty but couldn't be bothered with loads of faff. The chicken's simply seasoned (just garlic granules, nothing fancy), but once it's layered up with cream cheese, pesto and crispy halloumi, it all just *works*. Toasting the wrap at the end makes it feel a bit extra, even though it's dead easy.

1. Spray a large non-stick pan with oil and place over a medium to high heat. Add the chicken, garlic granules, salt and black pepper. Fry for 5–6 minutes, until golden and cooked through. Set aside.
2. In the same pan, fry the halloumi slices for 1–2 minutes each side, until golden. Set aside.
3. Mix the red pesto, mayo, Greek yoghurt and lemon juice in a small bowl.
4. For each wrap, make a single cut from the centre out to the bottom edge to help with folding (see page 157). Imagine the wrap in quarters, starting with the bottom left corner and working clockwise.
   - Spread 1 tbsp of cream cheese and 1 tsp of green pesto on the first quarter.
   - Add the chicken to the next.
   - Scatter the halloumi over the third.
   - Add rocket and a drizzle of the creamy red pesto sauce to the final quarter.
5. Fold the wrap up clockwise, one quarter at a time, into a triangle shape.
6. Wipe out the pan and spray with oil again. Toast the folded wraps for 1–2 minutes per side over a medium heat, until golden, warm and lightly crisp.

Sausage, Onion and Garlic Herb Cheese Baguette

SERVES 4 **CALORIES: 577**

Spray oil
8 pork sausages (approx. 400g), sliced
1 red onion, thinly sliced
3 tsp garlic purée (or 3 garlic cloves, grated)
100g garlic and herb cream cheese (I use Boursin)
4 soft sub rolls
Black pepper, to taste
Rocket or baby spinach, to serve (optional)

SWAPS

→ **Swap pork sausages for chicken sausages.** A leaner option that still packs flavour.
→ **Swap the cream cheese for a lighter version.** Keeps the creamy texture with fewer calories.
→ **Swap sub rolls for brioche buns.** A slightly sweet twist that works so well with the savoury filling.

This is one of those dinners that tastes like a total guilty pleasure, but it's surprisingly simple and quick. Fresh pasta means no waiting around, and everything gets tossed into one big cheesy, beefy hug of a dish. The kids demolish it. I usually make extra, and somehow it still disappears.

1. Spray a large pan with oil and place over a medium heat. Fry the sausage slices for 6–8 minutes, until golden and cooked through.
2. Add the red onion and cook for 3–4 minutes, until soft. Stir in the garlic and cook for 30 seconds.
3. Turn the heat to low, add the garlic and herb cream cheese, and stir until melted and creamy. Season with black pepper.
4. Slice open the rolls and fill with the sausage and cream cheese mix. Add rocket or baby spinach, if using, and serve.

SIDES

+ **Crispy potato wedges.** Bake a tray while you cook the filling for an easy fakeaway vibe.
+ **Quick slaw.** Mix grated carrot, cabbage and a dollop of light mayo or 0% Greek yoghurt for a crunchy side.
+ **Corn on the cob.** Microwave or grill for a buttery, juicy addition.

Piri Piri Halloumi and Pineapple Crunch Wraps

SERVES 4 **CALORIES: 654**

Spray oil
225g reduced-fat halloumi, sliced into strips
1 tbsp piri piri seasoning
4 pineapple rings (fresh or tinned), chopped
1 red pepper, finely sliced
4 large tortilla wraps
4 mini tortilla wraps (to use as the top layer)
60g lightly salted tortilla chips, crushed
Sweet chilli sauce, to drizzle

FOR THE SLAW
150g shredded white cabbage
1 small carrot, grated
2 tbsp light mayo
1 tsp white wine vinegar
Salt and black pepper, to taste

FOR THE PIRI PIRI MAYO
4 tbsp light mayo
1 tbsp piri piri seasoning
Juice of ½ a lime

Not to be dramatic... but these wraps might be one of the best things I've ever made. Spicy, cheesy, sweet, crunchy, they've got it all going on. And if your kids are anything like mine, the minute you call it a *crunch wrap*, they suddenly want three.

1. Spray a large pan with oil and place over a medium to high heat. Add the halloumi strips and cook for 2–3 minutes each side, until golden, then add the piri piri seasoning, pineapple and sliced pepper. Toss together and cook for 2–3 minutes, until caramelised and glossy.
2. Meanwhile, mix the slaw ingredients in a bowl and season to taste.
3. In a separate bowl, stir together the piri piri mayo ingredients.
4. Warm the large and mini wraps in the microwave to make them more flexible.
5. Now layer up: add slaw to the centre of each large wrap, then the piri piri halloumi, pineapple and peppers.
6. Top with the crushed tortilla chips, a drizzle of piri piri mayo, and finish with sweet chilli sauce.
7. Place a mini wrap on top and fold the edges of the large wrap up and over to seal.
8. Spray the pan again and put in the wraps, seam side down. Cook for 2–3 minutes each side, until golden and sealed.

SWAPS

→ **Swap halloumi for grilled chicken or tofu.** A simple swap that still packs flavour.
→ **Swap mayo for 0% Greek yoghurt in the sauce.** A lighter, tangier drizzle.
→ **Swap pineapple for grilled mango.** Still sweet but with a softer texture and slightly caramelised edges.

SIDES

+ **Serve with chilli potato wedges.** A bold side to match the flavours.
+ **Add corn ribs or grilled corn on the cob.** Sweet, smoky and fun to eat.

Cheesy & Indulgent

Mexican-style Chilli Cheese Rice

 GF **SERVES 4** **CALORIES: 597**

Spray oil
500g lean 5% beef mince
1 small onion, finely diced
1 pepper (any colour), diced
2 tsp garlic purée
1 tbsp tomato purée
2 tsp smoked paprika
2 tsp ground cumin
2 tsp mild chilli powder
1 tsp dried oregano
1 x 400g tin of chopped tomatoes
100g tinned kidney beans, drained (optional)
500g cold cooked basmati rice (2 microwave pouches)
60g chilli Cheddar, grated
60g full-fat mozzarella, grated
Salt and black pepper, to taste
A handful of fresh coriander, chopped

If you've followed me for a while, you'll know I'm a big fan of anything that involves melted cheese and minimal washing-up, and this one ticks both boxes. It's a proper shortcut chilli with a cheesy twist, stirred through fluffy rice and finished with gooey mozzarella and chilli Cheddar on top. No fuss, no faff... and not a single complaint from the kids.

1. Spray a large pan with oil and place over a medium to high heat. Add the beef mince, onion and pepper, and cook for 5–6 minutes until browned and softened.
2. Add the garlic, tomato purée, paprika, cumin, chilli powder, oregano, and a good pinch of salt and black pepper. Stir well and cook for 1 minute, until fragrant.
3. Pour in the chopped tomatoes and simmer for 2–3 minutes, until thickened slightly. Stir in the kidney beans, if using.
4. Add the cooked rice and stir through for 1–2 minutes, until piping hot.
5. Turn the heat to low, sprinkle over the chilli Cheddar and mozzarella, then cover the pan with a lid or foil for 1–2 minutes until the cheese has melted.
6. Finish with a handful of chopped coriander and serve hot.

SWAPS

→ **Swap beef mince for turkey or chicken mince.** A leaner option that still works beautifully.
→ **Swap kidney beans for black beans.** A richer flavour with a firmer bite.
→ **Swap chilli Cheddar for extra mature Cheddar.** A punchier cheese melt with less spice.

SIDES

+ **Tortilla chips.** Great for scooping and adding crunch.
+ **Chopped lettuce, tomato and cucumber.** Quick, fresh and cooling alongside the spice.
+ **Spoonful of sour cream or 0% Greek yoghurt.** Balances the heat and adds creaminess.

Cream Cheese and Chive Orzo

SERVES 4 **CALORIES: 512**

I've made a lot of creamy pasta dishes over the years, but this one's a bit of a hidden gem. It's simple, cosy and full of flavour, my kind of midweek magic. The orzo cooks right in the stock so it soaks up loads of flavour, then you stir through cream cheese, Cheddar and a handful of herbs and it turns into this silky, garlicky dream.

Spray oil
1 small onion, finely diced
4 tsp garlic purée
1 tsp onion granules
300g orzo
700ml hot chicken stock
Salt and black pepper (generous pinch of each)
½ tsp dried parsley
½ tsp dried chives
100ml semi-skimmed milk
100g light cream cheese
60g extra mature Cheddar, grated
2 tbsp fresh chives, finely chopped (plus extra to serve)

1. Spray a large pan with oil and place over a medium heat. Add the onion and cook for 2–3 minutes, until softened.
2. Stir in the garlic purée, onion granules and orzo. Cook for 1 minute, then pour in the hot chicken stock and season well with salt, black pepper, dried parsley and dried chives.
3. Simmer gently for 8–10 minutes, stirring often, until the orzo is tender and most of the liquid has been absorbed.
4. Lower the heat and stir in the milk, cream cheese, Cheddar and fresh chives. Keep stirring for 1–2 minutes, until silky and creamy.
5. Top with a few extra chives and serve straight away.

SWAPS

→ Swap Cheddar for grated full-fat mozzarella. Creamy and stretchy, with a milder flavour.
→ Swap chicken stock for veggie stock. Makes it vegetarian-friendly.
→ Swap orzo for small pasta shapes such as macaroni. Same vibe, slightly different texture.

SIDES

+ Crispy pancetta or bacon bits. To add crunch and a salty edge.
+ Tenderstem broccoli or green beans. Light, fresh veg to go on the side.
+ Ready-to-eat rocket with balsamic glaze. A peppery, sharp contrast to the creaminess.

Cheesy Mozzarella Chicken Flatbread Bake

SERVES 4 **CALORIES: 441**

Spray oil
500g chicken breast, diced
1 small onion, finely sliced
2 peppers (any colour), sliced
2 tsp garlic granules
1 tsp smoked paprika
1 tsp dried oregano
Salt and black pepper, to taste
200ml hot chicken stock
80ml single cream
2 plain flatbreads (approx. 120g each), chopped into large bite-size pieces
100g full-fat mozzarella, grated
Chilli flakes or chopped fresh parsley, to finish (optional)

This one was a bit of a happy accident... I had some flatbreads to use up and ended up throwing them straight into the pan with the chicken, peppers and a creamy garlicky sauce, then topped it all with mozzarella and let it melt down into this gooey, cheesy bake. It's somewhere between a flatbread pizza and a creamy chicken dish, and honestly, the kids were obsessed – barely a crumb left behind!

1. Spray a large pan with oil and place over a medium to high heat. Add the chicken, onion and peppers. Cook for 6–7 minutes, until the chicken is golden and the veg have softened.
2. Add the garlic granules, smoked paprika, oregano, salt and black pepper, and stir well to coat. Pour in the hot chicken stock and cream and let it bubble for 1–2 minutes, until the sauce starts to thicken slightly.
3. Add the chopped flatbreads and stir gently through until they have soaked up the sauce.
4. Top with the mozzarella, cover with a lid or foil, and cook for 2–3 minutes over a low heat until the cheese is melted and gooey.
5. Finish with chilli flakes or parsley, if you like, and serve hot.

SWAPS

→ **Swap chicken for turkey breast.** Lean, flavourful and just as quick to cook.
→ **Swap single cream for light cream cheese.** Creamy and still indulgent, with fewer calories.
→ **Swap mozzarella for Red Leicester.** Adds a rich colour and slightly sharper flavour.

SIDES

+ **Minted cucumber salad.** Fresh and cooling on the side.
+ **Ready-to-eat mixed leaf salad.** Zero prep and balances the richness.
+ **Microwave peas or green beans.** Quick, easy and they add colour to the plate.

Cheesy & Indulgent

Hot and Spicy Cheesy Ramen

SERVES 4 **CALORIES: 517**

This is one of those dinners that sounds a bit rogue – spicy ramen, melty cheese and gyozas all in one pan – but honestly, it works. My husband and Harry are both all about the spice, and even Lottie gets stuck in (as long as she's got a glass of milk on standby!). It's full of flavour, total fakeaway vibes, and the best bit? It's done in 15 minutes and uses only one pan... so I can actually sit down before the evening chaos kicks back in.

Spray oil
3 tsp garlic purée
3 tsp ginger purée
1 tbsp gochujang (Korean chilli paste)
1 tbsp soy sauce
1 tbsp honey
1 tsp chilli oil, plus extra to drizzle
800ml hot chicken or vegetable stock
200g ramen noodles (dried, or 4 instant noodle nests without seasoning)
80ml single cream
100g full-fat mozzarella, grated
40g Red Leicester, grated
8 frozen gyozas (any filling)
1 spring onion, sliced
Sesame seeds and chopped fresh coriander (optional)

1. Spray a large pan with oil and place over a medium heat. Add the garlic purée and ginger purée and cook for 1 minute, until fragrant.
2. Stir in the gochujang, soy sauce, honey and chilli oil. Cook for 30 seconds to warm through.
3. Pour in the hot stock and bring to a gentle simmer. Add the noodles and cook for 3–4 minutes until just tender, stirring often.
4. Stir through the cream, mozzarella and Red Leicester until melted and creamy.
5. Place the frozen gyozas on top, cover with a lid, and steam for 5 minutes until cooked through.
6. Top with spring onions, sesame seeds, coriander, if you like, and an optional extra drizzle of chilli oil.

SWAPS

→ **Swap cream for coconut milk.** Adds a slightly sweet twist and still keeps it rich.
→ **Swap gyozas for dumplings or wontons.** Equally delicious and steamy.
→ **Swap chilli oil for sriracha.** For a different kind of heat with a vinegary kick.

SIDES

+ **Cucumber ribbons with lime and sesame oil.** Bright and refreshing next to the heat.
+ **Edamame beans.** Quick and easy protein-packed side.
+ **Toasted sesame flatbread strips.** Great for scooping up the extra broth.

Chorizo and Red Leicester Gnocchi

SERVES 4   **CALORIES: 461**

Spray oil
100g diced chorizo
1 onion, finely diced
2 peppers (any colour), chopped
3 tsp garlic purée
2 tsp smoked paprika
1 tsp dried oregano
1 tsp onion granules
Salt and black pepper, to taste
1 tbsp tomato purée
100ml single cream
300ml hot chicken stock
500g gnocchi
80g Red Leicester, grated
40g full-fat mozzarella, grated
Chopped fresh parsley, to garnish (optional)

SWAPS

→ **Swap chorizo for smoked sausage.** Still brings the smoky flavour but slightly less rich.
→ **Swap single cream for light cream cheese.** Keeps it creamy but cuts down on calories.
→ **Swap gnocchi for fresh tortellini.** A cheesy twist with a similar cook time.

This one's full-on flavour in the best kind of way – smoky, creamy, a little bit spicy, and packed with that rich, savoury depth you only get from proper chorizo. The Red Leicester adds a mellow sharpness that works so well with the garlic and herbs, and the gnocchi soak it all up like little flavour sponges. It's one of those dinners that tastes like it's taken way longer than 15 minutes, and honestly, it always gets silence at the table, which is saying something in our house!

1. Heat a large frying pan over a medium heat and spray with oil. Add the chorizo and cook for 2–3 minutes, until crispy. Remove from the pan and set aside.
2. To the same pan, add the onion and peppers. Cook for 2–3 minutes, until softened. Stir in the garlic purée and cook for 1 minute.
3. Add the smoked paprika, oregano, onion granules, salt and black pepper. Stir through the tomato purée.
4. Pour in the cream and hot chicken stock, then add the gnocchi. Simmer for 4–5 minutes, stirring occasionally, until the gnocchi are tender and the sauce has thickened.
5. Stir in the crispy chorizo, leaving some to garnish, then sprinkle over the Red Leicester and mozzarella. Cover with a lid or foil for 1–2 minutes, until the cheese has melted, then garnish with the chorizo and the parsley, if using.

SIDES

+ **Roasted Mediterranean veg (frozen, oven or air fryer).** Adds colour, flavour and balances out the richness.
+ **Microwaved baby corn and sugar snap peas.** Crunchy, sweet, no prep needed and ready in minutes.
+ **Crusty seeded rolls.** Great for mopping up the cheesy sauce and adds a bit of texture.

Smoky Bacon, Garlic and Herb Alfredo

SERVES 4 **CALORIES: 460**

Spray oil
150g smoked bacon medallions, chopped
3 tsp garlic purée
10g unsalted butter
300ml hot chicken stock
500g fresh tagliatelle
150ml single cream
150g garlic and herb cream cheese (I use Boursin)
Salt and black pepper, to taste
Chopped fresh parsley, to serve (optional)

SWAPS

→ **Swap smoked bacon for cooked chicken pieces.** Still packed with flavour and ideal for using leftovers.
→ **Swap single cream for light cream cheese.** Keeps it creamy with fewer calories.
→ **Swap tagliatelle for fresh linguine.** A slightly thinner pasta that works just as well.

This one's dangerously good… the kind of dinner where everyone's silent at the table because they're too busy inhaling it. Smoky bacon, garlicky soft cheese, creamy pasta, it's got all the good stuff. No drama, just proper comfort food that tastes like a treat night but takes less time than arguing over what to watch on Netflix.

1. Spray a large pan with oil and place over a medium to high heat. Add the bacon and fry for 3–4 minutes, until golden and slightly crisp.
2. Stir in the garlic purée and butter, cooking for 1 minute until fragrant.
3. Pour in the hot chicken stock and bring to a gentle simmer. Add the fresh tagliatelle and use tongs to gently separate the strands as they soften. Simmer for 3–4 minutes, stirring occasionally.
4. Once the pasta is nearly cooked, pour in the cream and stir through the garlic and herb cream cheese until melted into a silky sauce. Let it bubble for a minute to thicken slightly. Season to taste with salt and black pepper.
5. Serve topped with a little chopped parsley, if you like.

SIDES

+ **Garlic and herb flatbreads (shop-bought).** Perfect for scooping up any extra sauce, a guaranteed crowd-pleaser.
+ **Steamed green beans or tenderstem broccoli (microwaved).** Adds fresh crunch and a bit of green to balance the richness.
+ **Crispy side salad with rocket and cherry tomatoes.** A light, peppery contrast that cuts through the creamy pasta beautifully.

'Nduja and Cheddar Rice

  SERVES 4 **CALORIES: 353**

Spray oil
1 onion, finely diced
2 peppers (any colour), diced
3 tsp garlic purée
3 tbsp 'nduja paste
1 tsp smoked paprika
1 tsp ground coriander
Salt and black pepper, to taste
300ml hot chicken stock
500g cold cooked basmati rice (2 microwave pouches)
100g extra mature Cheddar, grated
Chopped fresh parsley, to finish (optional)

If you're into bold flavours, this one's going to be a favourite. It's smoky, spicy, rich and cheesy, proper comfort food but with a little kick. The 'nduja brings that deep chilli warmth, the Cheddar melts through for creaminess, and the rice soaks it all up like a dream. It's the kind of dish that smells unreal while it's cooking and tastes even better. No boring bites, that's a bit of me.

1. Heat a large pan over a medium heat and spray with oil. Add the onion and peppers and cook for 3–4 minutes, until softened.
2. Stir in the garlic purée and 'nduja paste and cook for 2–3 minutes, letting the 'nduja melt into the pan and release all that smoky flavour.
3. Add the smoked paprika, ground coriander, salt and black pepper. Add the hot chicken stock and stir to combine.
4. Tip in the cooked rice and mix everything together. Let it simmer for 3–4 minutes, until heated through and the flavours are combined.
5. Stir through the grated Cheddar until melted. Finish with the chopped parsley, if using, and serve straight away.

SWAPS

→ **Swap 'nduja for harissa paste.** Still brings heat and depth but with a North African twist and no meat.
→ **Swap Cheddar for crumbled feta.** Adds a salty, tangy contrast that works beautifully with the spice.
→ **Swap basmati rice for cooked quinoa.** A high-protein, gluten-free base that soaks up all the flavour.

SIDES

+ **Ready-to-eat slaw.** Adds crunch and freshness to balance the heat.
+ **Steamed tenderstem broccoli (microwaved).** Light and green to cut through the richness.
+ **Crispy tortilla chips.** A fun scoop-and-eat option to make it feel like a treat.

Cheesy BBQ Sausage Rice

  SERVES 4   **CALORIES: 595**

Spray oil
6 gluten-free pork sausages, sliced into bite-size pieces
1 onion, finely diced
2 peppers (any colour), chopped
3 tsp garlic purée
4 tbsp BBQ sauce (plus extra to drizzle)
1 tbsp tomato purée
1 tbsp smoked paprika
1 tsp dried oregano
1 tsp onion granules
300ml hot chicken stock
500g cold cooked basmati rice (2 microwave pouches)
80g extra mature Cheddar, grated
80g full-fat mozzarella, grated
Salt and black pepper, to taste
Chopped fresh parsley, to finish

This is what I call a midweek crowd-pleaser – cheesy, sticky, BBQ sausage rice that looks like an effort but takes no time at all. The kind of dinner that has the kids asking for seconds and my husband thinking I've pulled out all the stops (spoiler: I haven't). One pan, barely any washing up... and loads of flavour. It's giving 'fakeaway night without the price tag' and I am absolutely here for it.

1. Spray a large pan with oil and place over a medium to high heat. Add the sliced sausages and cook for 4–5 minutes, until golden and cooked through.
2. Stir in the onion, peppers and garlic purée and cook for 2–3 minutes, until softened.
3. Add the BBQ sauce, tomato purée, smoked paprika, oregano, onion granules and seasoning. Stir well.
4. Pour in the hot chicken stock and bubble for 1 minute.
5. Stir through the cooked rice and heat for 2–3 minutes, until piping hot and everything's combined.
6. Scatter over the Cheddar and mozzarella, cover with a lid or foil and let the cheese melt for 1–2 minutes.
7. Drizzle with a little extra BBQ sauce and finish with chopped parsley.

SWAPS

→ **Swap pork sausages for smoky vegan sausages, chicken stock for veggie stock and cheese for vegan cheese.** Keeps that bold flavour and makes it plant-based.
→ **Swap mozzarella for Red Leicester.** Adds colour and a sharper cheese flavour.
→ **Swap BBQ sauce for chipotle BBQ.** A deeper, spicier flavour twist.

SIDES

+ **Microwaved corn on the cob.** Fast, sweet and buttery, perfect with BBQ sausage.
+ **Chopped salad with lime dressing.** Cuts through the richness and keeps it fresh.
+ **Mini garlic flatbreads.** Use them to scoop up every last cheesy bite.

Creamy Garlic Cheese Tortellini

SERVES 4 **CALORIES: 448**

Spray oil
1 small onion, finely diced
4 tsp garlic purée
1 tsp onion granules
300ml chicken stock (made with 1 stock cube)
500g fresh cheese tortellini
100ml single cream
100g garlic and herb cream cheese
60g extra mature Cheddar, grated
40g full-fat mozzarella, grated
1 tsp dried chives
1 tsp dried parsley
Salt and black pepper, to taste
A handful of fresh parsley, chopped, to garnish

There's just something about cheesy pasta that feels like a hug at the end of the day, isn't there? This one's got all the cosy vibes – melty cheese, soft tortellini, and a garlicky creamy sauce that comes together in one pot while you tidy up the day (or hide from the washing pile). It's the kind of dinner that makes everything feel a bit calmer.

1. Spray a large pan with oil and place over a medium heat. Add the onion and cook for 2–3 minutes, until soft. Stir in the garlic purée and onion granules, and cook for 30 seconds more.
2. Pour in the chicken stock and bring to a simmer. Add the tortellini and cook for 3–4 minutes, until tender.
3. Lower the heat and stir in the cream, garlic and herb cream cheese, Cheddar, mozzarella, chives and dried parsley. Let it bubble gently for 2–3 minutes, until the sauce thickens and coats the pasta.
4. Season to taste, garnish with the fresh parsley, and serve.

SWAPS

→ Swap chicken stock for **vegetable stock.** Easy way to make it veggie-friendly.
→ Swap Cheddar for **Red Leicester.** Adds a richer colour and a little sweetness.
→ Swap cheese tortellini for **spinach and ricotta.** A slightly lighter but still creamy option.

SIDES

+ **Garlic flatbreads.** Perfect for mopping up all that cheesy sauce.
+ **Simple rocket salad.** Adds a fresh bite to balance the creaminess.
+ **Microwaved green beans.** Quick and easy side for extra veg.

6-Cheese Mac 'n' Cheese

SERVES 4 **CALORIES: 575**

300g macaroni or short pasta
600ml hot chicken stock
300ml semi-skimmed milk
1 tsp English mustard (optional)
2 tsp garlic granules
Salt and black pepper, to taste
60g extra mature Cheddar, grated
40g Red Leicester, grated
60g full-fat mozzarella, grated
50g light cream cheese
20g Parmesan, finely grated, plus extra to serve (optional)
40g Monterey Jack, grated

If there's one dinner I know I can count on to keep the peace, it's mac 'n' cheese. My two are obsessed, like, proper scrape-the-bowl levels of obsession. This version's a little extra (in the best way), with six different cheeses and pasta cooked straight in chicken stock for loads of flavour. It feels like a big cheesy hug in a bowl. No whinging, no leftovers... just silence and cheesy faces.

1. Put the pasta and hot chicken stock into a large saucepan over a medium to high heat. Bring to a gentle boil and cook for 8–9 minutes, stirring often, until the pasta is almost tender and most of the liquid has been absorbed.
2. Reduce the heat to low. Stir in the milk, mustard, garlic granules, and a good pinch of salt and black pepper. Let it warm through for 1–2 minutes.
3. Add all the cheeses: Cheddar, Red Leicester, mozzarella, cream cheese, Parmesan and Monterey Jack. Stir gently for 1–2 minutes, until melted, glossy and coating the pasta beautifully.
4. Serve straight away, with a sprinkle of extra Parmesan, if you like!

SWAPS

→ **Swap chicken stock for veggie stock.** Keeps the flavour rich while making it vegetarian.
→ **Swap cream cheese for garlic and herb cream cheese.** Adds even more flavour with no extra effort.
→ **Swap Red Leicester for Double Gloucester.** Slightly milder but still creamy and colourful.

SIDES

+ **Toasted garlic flatbreads.** Fast, easy and perfect for scooping up every last bit.
+ **Microwaved broccoli florets.** They steam in minutes and add balance to the plate.
+ **Crispy salad with lemony dressing.** Sharp and fresh to cut through all that cheese.

Cheesy & Indulgent

Cheesy Honey Mustard Chicken and Potatoes

GF · **SERVES 4** · **CALORIES: 587**

Spray oil
500g chicken breast, diced
1 tsp garlic granules
500g tinned new potatoes, drained and sliced
1 tbsp unsalted butter
2 tbsp honey
2 tbsp Dijon mustard
200ml hot chicken stock
120g extra mature Cheddar, grated
1 tsp dried parsley (optional)
Salt and black pepper, to taste

SWAPS

- Swap chicken breast for reduced-fat halloumi chunks. Still gives that golden, savoury bite and works beautifully with honey and mustard.
- Swap Cheddar for Red Leicester. Adds extra colour and a mellow flavour.
- Swap Dijon mustard for wholegrain. For a milder, slightly sweeter tang.

This one's proper comfort food but still so easy to throw together. The chicken and potatoes get all golden in the pan, then you stir through that sweet, tangy, honey mustard sauce and finish it off with melty Cheddar. It's the kind of dinner everyone clears their plate for, and you won't even have loads to wash up afterwards!

1. Spray a large pan with oil and place over a medium to high heat. Add the chicken, garlic granules, salt and black pepper, and cook for 4–5 minutes, until browned.
2. Add the sliced potatoes and butter, and cook for another 3–4 minutes until golden. Stir in the honey, mustard and hot chicken stock, and let it bubble for 2 minutes until slightly reduced.
3. Sprinkle over the cheese, pop on a lid and let it melt into a gooey, golden topping.
4. Finish with dried parsley, if you like, and serve straight from the pan.

SIDES

+ **Serve with roasted carrots.** Naturally sweet and they pair beautifully with honey and mustard.
+ **Add steamed broccoli.** Brings colour and a fresh crunch.
+ **Serve with a simple rocket salad.** Peppery and light – great for cutting through the richness.

Ham and Cheese Croissant Bake

SERVES 4 **CALORIES: 517**

1 tbsp unsalted butter
1 tsp garlic purée
1 tsp Dijon mustard
1 tbsp plain flour
300ml semi-skimmed milk
180g extra mature Cheddar, grated
Salt and black pepper, to taste
4 all-butter croissants
4 slices of thick-cut ham
Chopped chives, to serve (optional)

SWAPS

→ Swap ham for cooked mushrooms or spinach. A great veggie option that still works with the rarebit flavours.
→ Swap Cheddar for Red Leicester. A slightly sweeter, colourful twist.
→ Swap Dijon for English mustard. For a bigger kick if you like it punchy.

This one's pure comfort: soft, buttery croissants stuffed with ham and cheese, all baked in a rich, cheesy sauce that soaks into the layers. It's like savoury bread and butter pudding meets Welsh rarebit, and it always goes down a treat. Perfect for a lazy brunch, quick tea, or those days when only something cheesy and golden will do.

1. Preheat the oven to 220°C/200°C fan.
2. In an ovenproof frying pan or shallow casserole, melt the butter over a medium heat.
3. Add the garlic and Dijon, then stir through the flour and cook for 30 seconds or so.
4. Gradually whisk in the milk until smooth, then add 60g of grated cheese. Stir until melted and season well.
5. Meanwhile, slice open the croissants and fill with the ham and the rest of the grated cheese. Nestle them into the pan on top of the sauce. Spoon some sauce over the top of the croissants to help it soak in.
6. Transfer the whole pan to the oven and bake for 8–10 minutes, until golden, bubbling and crisp on top.
7. Sprinkle with chives, if you fancy, and serve warm.

SIDES

+ Serve with rocket and balsamic salad. Adds a peppery contrast to the creamy bake.
+ Add some pickles. Sharp, crunchy and they cut through the richness.
+ Pair with roasted vine tomatoes. Soft, sweet and perfect on the side.

Sweet & Simple

Cookie Dough

❄ V **SERVES 4** **CALORIES: 391**

50g unsalted butter
3 tbsp light brown sugar
2 tbsp caster sugar
1 tsp vanilla extract
3 tbsp semi-skimmed milk
100g plain flour
A pinch of salt
80g milk chocolate chips

This one's a proper treat-yourself moment... warm, gooey cookie dough cooked in a pan and served straight to the table with melty ice cream on top. It's the kind of dessert that makes the whole family suddenly appear in the kitchen asking if they can 'just try a bit'. Dangerously easy. Ridiculously good. You've been warned.

1. Melt the butter in a frying pan over a medium heat, then turn off the heat. Stir in the sugars and the vanilla until combined, then add the milk.
2. Mix in the flour and a pinch of salt until you've got a thick dough. Fold through most of the chocolate chips, keeping a few back for the top.
3. Flatten out the dough in the pan and scatter over the remaining chocolate chips. Cook over a low heat for 5–6 minutes with a lid on, until the edges are just set but the middle stays soft.

SWAPS

→ **Swap milk chocolate for dark or white.** Use your fave or mix them for triple chocolate cookie vibes.
→ **Swap plain flour for oat flour.** Adds a slightly nutty flavour and a softer texture.
→ **Swap vanilla extract for almond or caramel.** A subtle flavour twist that's delish with chocolate.

SIDES

+ **Top with vanilla ice cream.** Classic combo that melts into the warm cookie.
+ **Add a drizzle of caramel sauce.** That rich, buttery sweetness pairs so well with the cookie.
+ **Serve with fresh strawberries or raspberries.** A little fruit cuts through the richness perfectly.

Caramelised Banana Pancakes

V | **SERVES 4** | **CALORIES: 336**

Spray oil
2 bananas (ripe but not mushy), sliced
2 tbsp light brown sugar
1 tsp ground cinnamon
1 tsp vanilla extract
150g plain flour
1½ tsp baking powder
1 tbsp caster sugar
A pinch of salt
1 egg
200ml semi-skimmed milk
1 tbsp unsalted butter, for frying
Maple syrup, to serve (optional)

These caramelised banana pancakes are what I make when I'm craving something sweet and cosy but don't want to go full-on with a big dessert. They're soft, golden and stacked up with warm, sticky bananas and a drizzle of sauce, basically the kind of pud that feels a bit indulgent but is still easy enough to throw together after dinner. Perfect for using up those overripe bananas, too... if they haven't already been claimed for smoothies or banana bread!

1. Spray a large pan with oil and place over a medium heat. Add the sliced bananas, sprinkle with brown sugar and cinnamon and drizzle in the vanilla. Cook for 2–3 minutes, until golden and caramelised, turning gently halfway through. Transfer to a plate and set aside.
2. In a bowl, mix the flour, baking powder, caster sugar and salt. Crack in the egg, pour in the milk, and whisk to a smooth batter.
3. Add the butter to the same large pan you used for the bananas, then spoon in dollops of the pancake batter (you should get around 8). Cook for 2–3 minutes on one side until bubbles form, then flip and cook for 1–2 minutes more.
4. Serve the pancakes stacked with the caramelised bananas on top and a drizzle of maple syrup, if you fancy.

SWAPS

→ **Swap plain flour for self-raising flour.** Slightly fluffier pancakes, with less need to measure baking powder.
→ **Swap cow's milk for oat or almond milk.** Keeps it dairy-free while still lovely and creamy.
→ **Swap bananas for peaches or plums.** Brings a summery twist with the same caramelised goodness.

SIDES

+ **A drizzle of warm speculoos spread or chocolate hazelnut spread.** Takes the flavour up a notch with that melty, rich topping.
+ **A dollop of Greek yoghurt and a handful of berries.** Adds a tangy, creamy contrast and makes it feel a bit lighter.
+ **Toasted coconut flakes and a squeeze of lime.** For a tropical twist that cuts through the sweetness beautifully.

Crispy Apple Charlotte

V   **SERVES 4**   **CALORIES: 212**

Spray oil or 1 tbsp unsalted butter

80g chunky breadcrumbs (I blend white sourdough)

1 tbsp caster sugar

Zest of ½ a lemon

4 apples (I use 2 Bramley and 2 Pink Lady), peeled and thinly sliced

1 tsp ground cinnamon

1 tbsp soft light brown sugar

Juice of ½ a lemon

This one takes me straight back to being little. My mum always made apple Charlotte, and the smell of the apples cooking with cinnamon is just pure comfort. I've put my own speedy spin on it, still warm and cosy, but all done in one pan and ready in minutes. Golden, crunchy breadcrumbs on top, soft apples underneath... it's proper childhood pudding vibes.

1. Spray a large pan with oil or melt the butter and toast the breadcrumbs with the caster sugar for 3–4 minutes, stirring regularly until golden and crisp. Add the lemon zest, then tip the crumbs out onto a plate.
2. Add the apples to the pan with the cinnamon, brown sugar and lemon juice. Cook for 6–8 minutes over a medium heat until soft and slightly sticky.
3. Sprinkle the golden breadcrumbs over the top and warm through for 1–2 minutes. Serve straight from the pan.

SWAPS

→ **Swap crispy breadcrumbs for crushed digestive biscuits.** Adds a buttery crunch and richer flavour.

→ **Swap Pink Lady apples for pears.** Keeps the sweetness but with a softer bite.

→ **Swap brown sugar for maple syrup.** Adds a subtle caramel flavour and glossy finish.

SIDES

+ **Warm custard.** Classic comfort and perfect for cold evenings.
+ **Scoop of vanilla ice cream.** Melts into the hot apples and adds creaminess.
+ **0% Greek yoghurt with a drizzle of honey.** A tangy, lighter option that still feels indulgent.

Pistachio S'mores Dip

V   **SERVES 4**   **CALORIES: 491**

150g milk chocolate, broken into chunks
4 tbsp pistachio spread
100g marshmallows (use vegetarian, if needed)
Digestive biscuits, to serve

This is one of those desserts that looks impressive but takes no time at all, and honestly, it's ridiculously good. That gooey marshmallow top, the melty chocolate base and the surprise layer of pistachio spread... trust me, it's a game-changer. Grab a digestive, get dipping, and try not to eat the whole lot in one go (I failed).

1. Preheat your oven to 200°C/180°C fan. Arrange the milk chocolate chunks in an even layer across the bottom of an ovenproof dish.
2. Spoon the pistachio spread over the top, dotting it around. Top with the marshmallows, covering the surface completely.
3. Bake in the oven for 6–8 minutes, until the chocolate is melted and the marshmallows are golden and gooey on top.
4. Serve immediately, with digestive biscuits for dipping.

SWAPS

→ **Swap milk chocolate for dark or white chocolate.** To change up the sweetness level and flavour profile.
→ **Swap pistachio spread for speculoos spread or chocolate hazelnut spread.** A different kind of nutty or spiced twist.
→ **Swap digestives for waffle cones or strawberries.** Adds crunch or a fruity contrast.

SIDES

+ **Add crushed pistachios on top after baking.** For extra crunch and to make it look the part.
+ **Serve with shortbread fingers or pretzel sticks.** Sweet or salty dippers work brilliantly here.
+ **Use mini cast-iron pans to make individual portions.** Great for parties or date nights.

Cheesecake French Toast

V | **SERVES 4** | **CALORIES: 297**

- 150g light cream cheese
- 1½ tbsp icing sugar, plus extra to serve (optional)
- 1 tsp vanilla extract
- 4 thick slices of brioche bread
- 2 large eggs
- 100ml semi-skimmed milk
- ½ tsp ground cinnamon
- 1 tsp caster sugar
- Spray oil
- 1 tbsp unsalted butter
- Maple syrup, to serve (optional)

This one's for those mornings when you want something a bit indulgent without going full dessert-for-breakfast mode (but we're definitely halfway there). Think soft golden brioche, creamy vanilla cheesecake filling and a hint of cinnamon, all cooked in one pan. It's giving Sunday brunch, but make it effortless. Perfect with a coffee and a quiet five minutes to yourself... or shared with the kids if you're feeling generous.

1. In a bowl, mix the cream cheese, icing sugar and vanilla until smooth.
2. Cut a slit in each brioche slice to form a pocket, and fill each one with the cream cheese mix.
3. In another bowl, whisk together the eggs, milk, cinnamon, and caster sugar.
4. Spray a large pan with oil and place over a medium heat. Dip each stuffed brioche slice into the egg mixture, making sure it soaks it up well on both sides.
5. Add the butter to the pan, then cook the French toast for 2–3 minutes per side until golden and crispy.
6. Serve with a dusting of icing sugar and a drizzle of maple syrup, if you like.

SWAPS

- → **Swap brioche for hot cross buns.** Adds a spiced fruity twist that's great for weekend brunch.
- → **Swap cream cheese for ricotta.** Lighter texture with a slightly savoury note.
- → **Swap cinnamon for nutmeg.** Adds a warm, slightly sweet depth of flavour.

SIDES

+ **Fresh berries.** They add natural sweetness and colour to the plate.
+ **Greek yoghurt.** Creamy, tangy and balances out the richness.
+ **Crispy bacon.** Sweet and salty combo that hits every time.

Sweet & Simple

Cheat's Sticky Toffee Pudding

V **SERVES 4** **CALORIES: 362**

100g pitted dates, chopped up small
100ml boiling water
½ tsp bicarbonate of soda
40g unsalted butter
50g soft light brown sugar
1 tsp vanilla extract
1 egg
75g self-raising flour
A pinch of salt
100g ready-made toffee sauce

SWAPS

→ **Swap self-raising flour for almond flour + ½ tsp baking powder.** Adds a nutty flavour and makes it naturally gluten-free (just check the baking powder is GF).

→ **Swap light brown sugar for coconut sugar.** Adds a deeper, almost caramel-like richness and is a less-refined option.

→ **Swap toffee sauce for light caramel dessert topping.** A lower-calorie option that still gives that sticky-sweet hit.

This one takes me straight back to Sunday dinners growing up, that moment when someone mentions pudding and everyone suddenly finds room! Sticky toffee has always been my husband's absolute favourite, so I had to come up with a quicker version we could enjoy without the wait. This cheat's take is super quick and still has that rich, nostalgic flavour that makes it feel like a proper treat. Perfect for when you want a cosy pud *right now*.

1. Start by soaking the dates. Put them into a bowl with the boiling water and bicarbonate of soda and leave to soften for 5 minutes. Then mash well with a fork.
2. Meanwhile, place a small ovenproof pan (approx. 20cm) over a medium heat. Add the butter and brown sugar, stirring until melted. Remove from the heat and leave to cool slightly.
3. Add the mashed dates, vanilla and egg, and mix well. Fold in the flour and salt until just combined.
4. Smooth out the batter in the pan. Cover loosely with foil or a lid and cook over a low heat for 8 minutes, until puffed up and set. If the top is still a little soft, finish under a medium grill for 2–3 minutes, until golden and bubbling. Add the toffee sauce just before the end.
5. Serve warm, with your favourite side (see below!).

SIDES

+ **Vanilla ice cream.** Melts into the hot sponge for the ultimate combo.
+ **Custard.** Brings nostalgic, cosy vibes to every bite.
+ **0% Greek yoghurt.** Adds creaminess and balances the sweetness perfectly.

Speculoos Brownie

 V **SERVES 4** **CALORIES: 446**

50g unsalted butter
50g dark chocolate, chopped finely
100g soft light brown sugar
2 medium eggs
1 tsp vanilla extract
40g plain flour
2 tbsp cocoa powder
A pinch of salt
4 tbsp speculoos spread (I use Biscoff)
2 speculoos biscuits, crushed, plus extra to decorate

I don't know about you, but I've always got room for dessert… especially when it's warm, gooey, and smothered in speculoos spread (Biscoff is my preferred choice!). This one-pot brownie is dangerously easy – think rich chocolate, swirls of speculoos, and that molten middle that's just begging for a scoop of ice cream (or custard… or cream… or why not all three?). It's an absolute crowd-pleaser, if you're willing to share.

1. Heat a pan over a low heat and add the butter and dark chocolate. Stir until fully melted and glossy, then remove from the heat and allow to cool slightly.
2. Stir in the sugar, then whisk in the eggs and vanilla extract until smooth.
3. Add the flour, cocoa powder and salt, and fold through gently until just combined – don't overmix.
4. Flatten the top and cook over a low heat for 6–7 minutes with a lid on. Halfway through, spoon in 3 tablespoons of the speculoos spread and gently swirl it through the brownie batter, then put the lid back on and cook until the edges are set but the middle is still soft and gooey.
5. Pop under the grill for 2–3 minutes, if needed.
6. Drizzle over the last tablespoon of speculoos spread and sprinkle with the crushed speculoos biscuits.
7. Serve warm, straight from the pan.

SWAPS

- → Swap dark chocolate for milk chocolate. Makes it sweeter and more indulgent.
- → Swap speculoos spread for chocolate hazelnut spread or peanut butter. Still indulgent, with a totally different flavour profile.
- → Swap plain flour for almond flour. Adds a nutty richness and makes it a little gooier.

SIDES

- + A scoop of vanilla ice cream. The hot brownie and cold ice cream combo is a match made in dessert heaven.
- + Warm custard poured over. Soaks in beautifully and adds that nostalgic, pudding-like feel.
- + A swirl of whipped cream. Balances the richness and adds a soft, fluffy finish.

Cherry and Chocolate Hazelnut Croissant Bake

V **SERVES 4** **CALORIES: 443**

Spray oil
4 all-butter croissants, halved lengthways
4 tbsp chocolate hazelnut spread (I use Nutella), plus extra to drizzle
4 tbsp cherry jam
2 medium eggs
100ml double cream
1 tsp vanilla extract
1 tbsp caster sugar
1 tsp icing sugar (optional), to dust

SWAPS

→ **Swap chocolate hazelnut spread for white chocolate spread.** Sweeter and creamier, pairs beautifully with cherry.
→ **Swap cherry jam for raspberry jam.** A tangy, vibrant twist.
→ **Swap croissants for brioche rolls.** Slightly fluffier texture, still buttery and rich.

Cherry and chocolate is my ultimate combo, I'll pick it over anything else every time. So this bake is basically my dream pud. Buttery croissants stuffed with chocolate hazelnut spread and cherry jam, soaked in vanilla custard and baked until golden and gooey. It's rich, sweet and ridiculously easy, the kind of dessert that feels a bit fancy but takes no time at all. Ideal for sharing (or not!).

1. Spray a large ovenproof frying pan or skillet with oil. Spread the cut sides of each croissant with chocolate hazelnut spread and a spoonful of cherry jam, then sandwich them back together and place in the pan.
2. In a jug, whisk the eggs, cream, vanilla and sugar, then pour over the croissants. Press down gently and leave for a minute to soak.
3. Warm over a low heat for 2 minutes while you preheat the grill to medium-high.
4. Pop under the grill for 5–6 minutes, until puffed up, golden and just set (watching so it doesn't catch and burn).
5. Finish with a drizzle of chocolate hazelnut spread and a dusting of icing sugar, if you like.

SIDES

+ **Scoop of vanilla ice cream.** Melts into the bake for extra indulgence.
+ **Dollop of thick 0% Greek yoghurt.** Adds a cooling, creamy contrast.
+ **Scatter of fresh cherries.** Brightens things up and adds freshness.

Rocky Road Melt

V | **SERVES 4** | **CALORIES: 585**

- 125g milk chocolate
- 125g dark chocolate
- 2 tbsp unsalted butter
- 2 tbsp golden syrup
- 60g mini marshmallows (use vegetarian, if needed)
- 60g digestive biscuits, broken into chunks
- 40g glacé cherries or dried cranberries
- 40g mini fudge pieces or chopped fudge bar

If there's one dessert that guarantees silence in our house (apart from the odd 'Mmm!'), it's this rocky road melt. The kids go wild for it, and I'm not far behind to be honest. It's gooey, chocolatey, and packed with all their favourites... and the best bit? It's all done in one pan in 15 minutes. Perfect for movie nights, rainy days or just when you need a quick win after dinner.

1. Put both chocolates, the butter and the golden syrup into a frying pan or shallow saucepan over a low heat. Stir gently until smooth and melted.
2. Once melted, turn off the heat and stir in the marshmallows, broken biscuits, cherries or cranberries and fudge pieces.
3. Fold everything through until it's evenly coated in the chocolate.
4. Let it sit for a few minutes to thicken slightly, then serve warm, straight from the pan.

SWAPS

→ **Swap glacé cherries for raisins.** Adds a chewy texture and a sweet yet tart twist.
→ **Swap digestive biscuits for rich tea or shortbread.** For a more buttery or crisp crunch.
→ **Swap fudge pieces for chopped Mars bar or Rolos.** A gooier caramel hit.

SIDES

+ **Serve with a scoop of vanilla ice cream.** The contrast of hot and cold is unbeatable.
+ **Add fresh strawberries or raspberries on top.** Cuts through the richness.
+ **Drizzle with a little cream or 0% Greek yoghurt.** For a super indulgent, spoonable dessert.

Molten Chocolate Fudge Cake

V · **SERVES 4** · **CALORIES: 540**

40g unsalted butter
75g dark chocolate (I use 50%)
80g caster sugar
1 egg
25ml semi-skimmed milk
1 tsp vanilla extract
70g self-raising flour
30g cocoa powder
A pinch of salt
Chocolate chips to scatter on top (optional)

There's something about warm chocolate cake that fixes everything – tantrums, long days, and that never-ending pile of laundry. I threw this one together in one pan while the kids were bickering over what to watch, and by the time it was done, we were all sitting at the table with spoons in hand and not a peep from anyone. Bliss.

1. Put the butter and chocolate into a small pan (approx. 20cm) and melt gently over a medium heat, stirring until smooth.
2. Take off the heat and stir in the sugar. In a bowl, whisk together the egg, milk and vanilla and add to the pan.
3. Sift in the self-raising flour, cocoa powder and salt, then gently fold in until smooth.
4. Level out the mix, cover with a lid and cook over a low heat for 8–9 minutes, until set on the edges and soft in the centre.
5. If needed, pop under the grill for 2–3 minutes. Then add the chocolate chips, if using.
6. Leave to rest for a few minutes, then serve straight from the pan.

SWAPS

→ Swap caster sugar for light brown sugar. Adds a richer, toffee-like flavour.
→ Swap self-raising flour for almond flour + ½ tsp baking powder. Adds a nutty flavour and makes it naturally gluten-free (just check the baking powder is GF).
→ Swap dark chocolate for milk chocolate or a mix of both. A sweeter, creamier flavour, perfect for kids and those who prefer a milder chocolate hit.

SIDES

+ **Vanilla ice cream.** Melts perfectly into the warm sponge.
+ **Chopped strawberries or raspberries.** A sharp, fruity contrast to the richness.
+ **Spoonful of thick cream or custard.** Extra indulgence for pudding lovers.

Apple and Gingerbread Crumble

V — **SERVES 4** — **CALORIES: 262**

Spray oil
30g unsalted butter
3 apples, peeled, cored and thinly sliced (I use Bramley cooking apples)
2 tbsp light brown sugar
1 tsp ground cinnamon
½ tsp ground ginger
1 tbsp lemon juice
4 gingernut biscuits, crushed
50g rolled oats
1 tbsp plain flour
1 tbsp maple syrup or honey
a pinch of salt

This one's a bit of a childhood classic with a cosy little twist. I've taken the flavours of spiced gingerbread and warm apples and turned them into a proper pud that's quick enough for a weeknight treat but seriously comforting. It's one of those desserts where the smell alone will have everyone wandering into the kitchen before it's even done!

1. Spray a large pan with oil and melt the butter over a medium heat. Add the apples, brown sugar, cinnamon, ginger and lemon juice. Stir well and cook for 5–6 minutes, until the apples soften and caramelise slightly.
2. Mix the crushed gingernuts in a bowl with the oats, flour, maple syrup or honey and a pinch of salt.
3. Sprinkle the crumble mixture evenly over the apples and cover with a lid. Leave to cook on a low heat for 2–3 minutes, then pop it under a hot grill to crisp up for another 2–3 minutes.
4. Serve warm, straight from the pan, with your favourite topping (see below).

SWAPS

→ **Swap gingernuts for digestive biscuits.** A milder flavour but still sweet and crumbly.
→ **Swap maple syrup for golden syrup.** Adds a deeper, richer sweetness.
→ **Swap oats for crushed cornflakes.** Lighter and crunchier topping.

SIDES

+ **Cinnamon ice cream.** A warm-meets-cold combo that brings out the ginger and apple flavours.
+ **Hot vanilla custard.** Silky, simple and nostalgic, perfect with the spiced crumble.
+ **Toasted pecans or walnuts.** Adds crunch and a nutty contrast to the soft crumble.

Lemon and Blueberry Brioche Pudding

V   **SERVES 4**   **CALORIES: 532**

Spray oil or unsalted butter, for greasing
250g brioche bread, roughly torn or sliced
100g lemon curd
100g blueberries (fresh or frozen)
2 eggs
200ml whole milk
100ml single cream
1 tsp vanilla extract
2 tbsp caster sugar
Zest of 1 lemon
Icing sugar, to dust (optional)

SWAPS

→ **Swap brioche for croissants.** A buttery twist that's equally indulgent.
→ **Swap lemon curd for raspberry jam.** Adds a sharp fruity contrast.
→ **Swap blueberries for mixed berries.** A colourful mix that works beautifully with lemon.

If you've ever bought a fancy brioche loaf for 'breakfast' and then totally forgotten about it… this one's for you. It's the perfect excuse to turn those sweet, buttery slices into something a bit magical. A zesty, gooey, custardy bake packed with lemon curd and bursting blueberries, like sunshine in dessert form.

1. Grease a large non-stick ovenproof pan with spray oil or butter. Add the brioche to the pan, dotting the lemon curd and blueberries in between the pieces.
2. In a bowl, whisk together the eggs, milk, cream, vanilla, sugar and lemon zest. Pour the mixture evenly over the brioche and gently press it down so it soaks in.
3. Place the pan over a medium heat for 5–6 minutes, covered with a lid or foil, and cook until the liquid has mostly been absorbed. Place under the grill for 2–3 minutes, until golden and just set in the centre.
4. Dust with icing sugar, if using, and serve warm.

SIDES

+ **Serve with crème fraîche.** Adds a little tang to balance the sweetness.
+ **Drizzle with warm white chocolate.** For an extra indulgent treat.
+ **Add a handful of flaked almonds on top.** Toasts beautifully under the grill for crunch and nuttiness.

Index

A
apples: apple and gingerbread crumble *211*
   crispy apple Charlotte *197*

B
bacon: chicken, bacon and tarragon pot pie *34*
   chicken, bacon and tomato rice *124*
   chicken Caesar folded wraps *156*
   creamy garlic and herb bacon ravioli *105*
   hunter's chicken sausages and Mediterranean veggies *23*
   pepperoni and pesto orzo *101*
   smoky bacon, garlic and herb alfredo *178*
   sweet chilli chicken and bacon wrap *149*
bananas: caramelised banana pancakes *195*
BBQ sauce: cheesy BBQ sausage rice *182*
   Korean BBQ beef and kimchi slaw pittas *159*
   lazy BBQ beef enchiladas *146*
beans: Tuscan chicken and chorizo beans *84*
   see also individual types of beans
beef: beef and butterbean stroganoff *30*
   burger loaded pittas *152*
   cheat's lasagne *27*
   cheeseburger pasta *47*
   hoisin sticky beef fried rice *118*
   Korean BBQ beef and kimchi slaw pittas *159*
   lazy BBQ beef enchiladas *146*
   loaded steak nachos *54*
   Mexican-style chilli cheese rice *169*
   Philly cheese steak sub *61*
   quick sloppy Joe toasties *155*
   red pesto beef pasta *100*
   sticky Chinese beef lettuce wraps *57*
   veg-packed spaghetti Bolognese *20*
blueberries: lemon and blueberry brioche pudding *212*
Bolognese, veg-packed spaghetti *20*
bread: honey mustard sausage baguette *82*
   loaded veg and pepperoni baguette pizza *144*
   meatball marinara subs *29*
   Philly cheese steak sub *61*
   quick sloppy Joe toasties *155*
   sausage, onion and garlic herb cheese baguette *163*
   see also flatbreads; pitta breads
brioche: cheesecake French toast *201*
   lemon and blueberry brioche pudding *212*
brownies, speculoos *204*
buffalo chicken quesadillas *58*
burger loaded pittas *152*
burger sauce *152*
butter chicken loaded naan *160*
butterbeans: beef and butterbean stroganoff *30*
   chorizo and butterbean rice *139*

C
cabbage: slaws *29*, *155*, *165*
Caesar sauce *156*
Cajun prawn alfredo pasta *108*
Cajun sausage rice salad, smoked *131*
cake, molten chocolate fudge *208*
caramelised banana pancakes *195*
carrots: crunchy slaw *29*
Charlotte, crispy apple *197*
cheat's fish and chips *66*
cheat's lasagne *27*
cheat's sticky toffee pudding *202*
cheese *166–89*
   buffalo chicken quesadillas *58*
   burger loaded pittas *152*
   cheeseburger pasta *47*
   cheesy BBQ sausage rice *182*
   cheesy honey mustard chicken and potatoes *187*
   cheesy Mexican-style rice *128*
   cheesy mozzarella chicken flatbread bake *173*
   cheesy pea and pesto pasta *94*
   cheesy pork and tarragon gnocchi *71*
   chicken Caesar folded wraps *156*
   chicken, halloumi and pesto folded wrap *162*
   chorizo and Red Leicester gnocchi *177*
   creamy garlic and Parmesan rice *134*
   creamy garlic cheese tortellini *184*
   creamy harissa and halloumi orzo *98*
   ham and cheese croissant bake *188*
   hot and spicy cheesy ramen *174*
   Mexican-style chilli cheese rice *169*
   'nduja and Cheddar rice *181*
   Philly cheese steak sub *61*
   piri piri halloumi and pineapple crunch wraps *165*
   quick sloppy Joe toasties *155*
   6-cheese mac 'n' cheese *185*
   veg and halloumi shakshuka *36*
   see also cream cheese
cheeseburger pasta *47*
cheesecake French toast *201*
cherries: rocky road melt *207*
cherry jam: cherry and chocolate hazelnut croissant bakes *205*
chicken: buffalo chicken quesadillas *58*
   butter chicken loaded naan *160*
   cheesy honey mustard chicken and potatoes *187*
   cheesy Mexican-style rice *128*
   cheesy mozzarella chicken flatbread bake *173*
   chicken, bacon and tarragon pot pie *34*
   chicken, bacon and tomato rice *124*
   chicken, halloumi and pesto folded wrap *162*
   chicken, ham and stuffing crumble *73*
   chicken Caesar folded wraps *156*
   chicken chow mein *33*
   chicken korma rice *46*
   chicken tikka and mango flatbreads *143*
   Coronation chicken and potatoes *35*
   creamy garlic and herb lasagne *83*
   garlic butter chicken rice *75*

marry me chicken rice *117*
quick souvlaki rice *87*
salt and pepper chicken stir-fry *45*
satay chicken rice *121*
smoky chicken and pineapple rice *137*
smoky chicken fajitas *24*
sweet and sour chicken rice *53*
sweet chilli chicken and bacon wrap *149*
Tuscan chicken and chorizo beans *84*
chilli sauce: sweet chilli chicken and bacon wrap *149*
chillies: garlic, chilli and ginger prawn rice *122*
honey garlic and chilli ramen *79*
Mexican-style chilli cheese rice *169*
Chinese beef lettuce wraps, sticky *57*
chips, cheat's fish and *66*
chocolate: cookie dough *192*
molten chocolate fudge cake *208*
pistachio s'mores dip *198*
rocky road melt *207*
speculoos brownie *204*
chocolate hazelnut spread:
cherry and chocolate hazelnut croissant bakes *205*
chorizo: cheesy Mexican-style rice *128*
chorizo and butterbean rice *139*
chorizo and Red Leicester gnocchi *177*
crispy chorizo and 'nduja pasta *97*
Tuscan chicken and chorizo beans *84*
chow mein, chicken *33*
cookie dough *192*
Coronation chicken and potatoes *35*
cream cheese: cheat's lasagne *27*
cheesecake French toast *201*
cheesy pea and pesto pasta *94*
chicken, halloumi and pesto folded wrap *162*
cream cheese and chive orzo *170*
creamy garlic and herb bacon ravioli *105*
creamy garlic and herb lasagne *83*
creamy garlic cheese tortellini *184*
creamy harissa and halloumi orzo *98*
creamy lemon and garlic ravioli *76*
gochujang and cream cheese pasta *111*
sausage, onion and garlic herb cheese baguette *163*
smoky bacon, garlic and herb alfredo *178*
croissants: cherry and chocolate hazelnut croissant bakes *205*
ham and cheese croissant bake *188*
crumbles: apple and gingerbread crumble *211*
chicken, ham and stuffing crumble *73*
curry: butter chicken loaded naan *160*
chicken korma rice *46*
lamb tikka masala *39*
smoked fish and sweetcorn curry *81*
Thai red curry noodles *50*

D
dates: cheat's sticky toffee pudding *202*
digestive biscuits: pistachio s'mores dip *198*
rocky road melt *207*
dip, pistachio s'mores *198*
doner kebabs, lamb *49*

E
eggs: cheesecake French toast *201*
veg and halloumi shakshuka *36*
enchiladas, lazy BBQ beef *146*
equipment *9, 13*

F
fajitas, smoky chicken *24*
fish: cheat's fish and chips *66*
fish pie gnocchi *40*
smoked fish and sweetcorn curry *81*
tuna crunch pasta salad *107*
flatbreads: cheesy mozzarella chicken flatbread bake *173*
chicken tikka and mango flatbreads *143*
freezing food *10*
French toast, cheesecake *201*
fudge: rocky road melt *207*
fudge cake, molten chocolate *208*

G
garlic: creamy garlic and Parmesan rice *134*
creamy lemon and garlic ravioli *76*
garlic butter chicken rice *75*
garlic, chilli and ginger prawn rice *122*
garlic yoghurt mayo *49*
honey garlic and chilli ramen *79*   lemon, garlic and thyme pasta *113*
garlic and herb cream cheese: creamy garlic cheese tortellini *184*
creamy garlic and herb bacon ravioli *105*
creamy garlic and herb lasagne *83*
sausage, onion and garlic herb cheese baguette *163*
smoky bacon, garlic and herb alfredo *178*
ginger: apple and gingerbread crumble *211*
garlic, chilli and ginger prawn rice *122*
gnocchi: cheesy pork and tarragon gnocchi *71*
chorizo and Red Leicester gnocchi *177*
fish pie gnocchi *40*
spicy sausage and pesto gnocchi *72*
gochujang (Korean chilli paste): gochujang and cream cheese pasta *111*
sticky gochujang pork rice *132*
green beans: spicy Szechuan pork and green bean stir-fry *62*
gyozas: hot and spicy cheesy ramen *174*

H

haddock, smoked: smoked fish and sweetcorn curry 81
ham: chicken, ham and stuffing crumble 73
    ham and cheese croissant bake 188
harissa: creamy harissa and halloumi orzo 98
hash, smoked sausage and sweet potato 88
hazelnut spread: cherry and chocolate hazelnut
    croissant bakes 205
hoisin sticky beef fried rice 118
honey: cheesy honey mustard chicken and
    potatoes 187
    honey garlic and chilli ramen 79
    honey mustard sausage baguette 82
hot and spicy cheesy ramen 174
hunter's chicken sausages and Mediterranean
    veggies 23

I

ingredients 10

K

kebabs, lamb doner 49
Korean BBQ beef and kimchi slaw pittas 159
korma rice, chicken 46

L

lamb: lamb doner kebabs 49
    lamb pitta pockets with salad and minted yoghurt 151
    lamb tikka masala 39
lasagne: cheat's lasagne 27
    creamy garlic and herb lasagne 83
lazy BBQ beef enchiladas 146
leftovers 10
lemon curd: lemon and blueberry brioche pudding 212
lemons: creamy lemon and garlic ravioli 76
    lemon and oregano rice 135
    lemon, garlic and thyme pasta 113
lettuce: chicken Caesar folded wraps 156
    sticky Chinese beef lettuce wraps 57
loaded steak nachos 54
loaded veg and pepperoni baguette pizza 144

M

mac 'n' cheese, 6-cheese 185
mango: chicken tikka and mango flatbreads 143
    fresh mango salsa 143
marinara subs, meatball 29
marry me chicken rice 117
marshmallows: pistachio s'mores dip 198
    rocky road melt 207
mayo: garlic yoghurt mayo 49
    piri piri mayo 165
    tartare sauce 66
meatball marinara subs 29
Mexican-style chilli cheese rice 169
Mexican-style rice, cheesy 128
minted yoghurt 143, 151
molten chocolate fudge cake 208
mustard: cheesy honey mustard chicken and
    potatoes 187
    honey mustard sausage baguette 82

N

naan, butter chicken loaded 160
nachos, loaded steak 54
'nduja: crispy chorizo and 'nduja pasta 97
    'nduja and Cheddar rice 181
    sausage and 'nduja rice 127
noodles: chicken chow mein 33
    honey garlic and chilli ramen 79
    hot and spicy cheesy ramen 174
    prawn pad Thai style noodles 65
    Thai red curry noodles 50

O

onions: sausage, onion and garlic herb
    cheese baguette 163
orzo: cream cheese and chive orzo 170
    creamy harissa and halloumi orzo 98
    pepperoni and pesto orzo 101

P

pad Thai style noodles, prawn 65
pancakes, caramelised banana 195
pans 9, 13
pasta 90–113
    Cajun prawn alfredo pasta 108
    cheat's lasagne 27
    cheeseburger pasta 47
    cheesy pea and pesto pasta 94
    cream cheese and chive orzo 170
    creamy garlic and herb bacon ravioli 105
    creamy garlic and herb lasagne 83
    creamy garlic cheese tortellini 184
    creamy harissa and halloumi orzo 98
    creamy lemon and garlic ravioli 76
    creamy sun-dried tomato tortellini 112
    crispy chorizo and 'nduja pasta 97
    gochujang and cream cheese pasta 111
    lemon, garlic and thyme pasta 113
    pepperoni and pesto orzo 101
    red pesto beef pasta 100
    roasted red pepper and sausage pasta 102
    6-cheese mac 'n' cheese 185
    smoked sausage and pepper tortellini 93
    smoky bacon, garlic and herb alfredo 178
    tuna crunch pasta salad 107
    veg-packed spaghetti Bolognese 20
peanut butter: prawn pad Thai style noodles 65
    satay chicken rice 121
peas: cheesy pea and pesto pasta 94
pepperoni: loaded veg and pepperoni baguette
    pizza 144
    pepperoni and pesto orzo 101
peppers: roasted red pepper and sausage pasta 102
    smoked sausage and pepper tortellini 93
pesto: cheesy pea and pesto pasta 94
    chicken, halloumi and pesto folded wrap 162
    pepperoni and pesto orzo 101
    red pesto beef pasta 100
    spicy sausage and pesto gnocchi 72
Philly cheese steak sub 61

pies: chicken, bacon and tarragon pot pie 34–41
   fish pie gnocchi 40
pineapple: piri piri halloumi and pineapple crunch wraps 165
   smoky chicken and pineapple rice 137
   sweet and sour chicken rice 53
piri piri halloumi and pineapple crunch wraps 165
pistachio s'mores dip 198
pitta breads: burger loaded pittas 152
   Korean BBQ beef and kimchi slaw pittas 159
   lamb doner kebabs 49
   lamb pitta pockets with salad and minted yoghurt 151
pizza, loaded veg and pepperoni baguette 144
pork: cheesy pork and tarragon gnocchi 71
   spicy Szechuan pork and green bean stir-fry 62
   sticky gochujang pork rice 132
   see also sausages
potatoes: cheat's fish and chips 66
   cheesy honey mustard chicken and potatoes 187
   Coronation chicken and potatoes 35
prawns: Cajun prawn alfredo pasta 108
   fish pie gnocchi 40
   garlic, chilli and ginger prawn rice 122
   prawn pad Thai style noodles 65
   Thai red curry noodles 50
puff pastry: chicken, bacon and tarragon pot pie 34

Q
quesadillas, buffalo chicken 58

R
ramen: honey garlic and chilli ramen 79
   hot and spicy cheesy ramen 174
ravioli: creamy garlic and herb bacon ravioli 105
   creamy lemon and garlic ravioli 76
reheating food 10
rice 114–39
   cheesy BBQ sausage rice 182
   cheesy Mexican-style rice 128
   chicken, bacon and tomato rice 124
   chicken korma rice 46
   chorizo and butterbean rice 139
   creamy garlic and Parmesan rice 134
   garlic butter chicken rice 75
   garlic, chilli and ginger prawn rice 122
   hoisin sticky beef fried rice 118
   lemon and oregano rice 135
   marry me chicken rice 117
   Mexican-style chilli cheese rice 169
   'nduja and Cheddar rice 181
   quick souvlaki rice 87
   satay chicken rice 121
   sausage and 'nduja rice 127
   smoked Cajun sausage rice salad 131
   smoky chicken and pineapple rice 137
   sticky gochujang pork rice 132
   sweet and sour chicken rice 53
rocky road melt 207

S
salads: slaws 29, 155, 165
   smoked Cajun sausage rice salad 131
   tuna crunch pasta salad 107
salsa, fresh mango 143
salt and pepper chicken stir-fry 45
satay chicken rice 121
sausages: cheesy BBQ sausage rice 182
   honey mustard sausage baguette 82
   hunter's chicken sausages and Mediterranean veggies 23
   roasted red pepper and sausage pasta 102
   sausage and 'nduja rice 127
   sausage, onion and garlic herb cheese baguette 163
   smoked Cajun sausage rice salad 131
   smoked sausage and pepper tortellini 93
   smoked sausage and sweet potato hash 88
   spicy sausage and pesto gnocchi 72
   see also chorizo
shakshuka, veg and halloumi 36
slaws 155
   crunchy slaw 29
   Korean BBQ beef and kimchi slaw pittas 159
   piri piri halloumi and pineapple crunch wraps 165
sloppy Joe toasties, quick 155
s'mores dip, pistachio 198
souvlaki rice, quick 87
spaghetti Bolognese, veg-packed 20
speculoos brownie 204
spicy sausage and pesto gnocchi 72
spicy Szechuan pork and green bean stir-fry 62
sticky Chinese beef lettuce wraps 57
sticky gochujang pork rice 132
sticky toffee pudding, cheat's 202
stir-fries: salt and pepper chicken stir-fry 45
   spicy Szechuan pork and green bean stir-fry 62
stroganoff, beef and butterbean 30
stuffing: chicken, ham and stuffing crumble 73
subs: meatball marinara subs 29
   Philly cheese steak sub 61
   sausage, onion and garlic herb cheese baguette 163
sweet and sour chicken rice 53
sweet chilli chicken and bacon wrap 149
sweet potatoes: smoked sausage and sweet potato hash 88
sweetcorn: smoked fish and sweetcorn curry 81
   tuna crunch pasta salad 107
Szechuan pork and green bean stir-fry, spicy 62

T
tartare sauce 66
Thai red curry noodles 50
tikka: chicken tikka and mango flatbreads 143
tikka masala, lamb 39
toasties, quick sloppy Joe 155
toffee sauce 202
tomatoes: chicken, bacon and tomato rice 124
   creamy sun-dried tomato tortellini 112
   marry me chicken rice 117
   meatball marinara subs 29
   veg and halloumi shakshuka 36
tortellini: creamy garlic cheese tortellini 184
   creamy sun-dried tomato tortellini 112
   smoked sausage and pepper tortellini 93
tortilla chips: loaded steak nachos 54
tortilla wraps: buffalo chicken quesadillas 58
   chicken Caesar folded wraps 156
   chicken, halloumi and pesto folded wrap 162
   lazy BBQ beef enchiladas 146
   piri piri halloumi and pineapple crunch wraps 165
tuna crunch pasta salad 107
Tuscan chicken and chorizo beans 84

V
vegetables: hunter's chicken sausages and Mediterranean veggies 23
   loaded veg and pepperoni baguette pizza 144
   veg and halloumi shakshuka 36
   veg-packed spaghetti Bolognese 20
   see also individual types of vegetables

W
wraps 140–65
   buffalo chicken quesadillas 58
   chicken Caesar folded wraps 156
   chicken, halloumi and pesto folded wrap 162
   chicken tikka and mango flatbreads 143
   lazy BBQ beef enchiladas 146
   piri piri halloumi and pineapple crunch wraps 165
   smoky chicken fajitas 24
   sticky Chinese beef lettuce wraps 57
   sweet chilli chicken and bacon wrap 149

Y
yoghurt: garlic yoghurt mayo 49
   minted yoghurt 143, 151

Conversion tables

WEIGHT	
METRIC	IMPERIAL
15g	½ oz
25g	1 oz
40g	1½ oz
50g	2 oz
75g	3 oz
100g	4 oz
150g	5 oz
175g	6 oz
200g	7 oz
225g	8 oz
250g	9 oz
275g	10 oz
350g	12 oz
375g	13 oz
400g	14 oz
425g	15 oz
450g	1 lb
550g	1¼ lb
675g	1½ lb
900g	2 lb
1.5kg	3 lb
1.75kg	4 lb
2.25kg	5 lb

VOLUME	
METRIC	IMPERIAL
25ml	1 fl oz
50ml	2 fl oz
85ml	3 fl oz
150ml	5 fl oz (¼ pint)
300ml	10 fl oz (½ pint)
450ml	1 fl oz (¾ pint)
600ml	1 pint
700ml	1¼ pints
900ml	1½ pints
1 litre	1¾ pints
1.2 litres	2 pints
1.25 litres	2¼ pints
1.5 litres	2½ pints
1.6 litres	2¾ pints
1.75 litres	3 pints
1.8 litres	3¼ pints
2 litres	3½ pints
2.1 litres	3¾ pints
2.25 litres	4 pints
2.75 litres	5 pints
3.4 litres	6 pints
3.9 litres	7 pints
5 litres	8 pints (1 gal)

MEASUREMENTS

METRIC	IMPERIAL
0.5cm	¼ inch
1cm	½ inch
2.5cm	1 inch
5cm	2 inches
7.5cm	3 inches
10cm	4 inches
15cm	6 inches
18cm	7 inches
20cm	8 inches
23cm	9 inches
25cm	10 inches
30cm	12 inches

OVEN TEMPERATURES

°C	FAN °C	°F	GAS MARK
140°C	120°C	275°F	Gas Mark 1
150°C	130°C	300°F	Gas Mark 2
160°C	140°C	325°F	Gas Mark 3
180°C	160°C	350°F	Gas Mark 4
190°C	170°C	375°F	Gas Mark 5
200°C	180°C	400°F	Gas Mark 6
220°C	200°C	425°F	Gas Mark 7
230°C	210°C	450°F	Gas Mark 8
240°C	220°C	475°F	Gas Mark 9

Acknowledgements

First and foremost, to my family – my mum and stepdad – thank you for passing on your love of food and cooking, and for being a constant support in everything I do.

To my children, Harry and Lottie – my biggest fans and my little guinea pigs, always taste-testing every recipe with so much enthusiasm. I love you both endlessly.

And to my husband – my rock. None of this would be possible without you. You've been by my side every step of the way and I'll never be able to thank you enough for the love, support and strength you give me every day.

To my amazing friends and family – thank you for always encouraging me, cheering me on and believing in me, even on the days I didn't believe in myself.

To my manager, Max – thank you for always being there at the end of the phone when I've felt overwhelmed and for helping me turn this dream into a reality. Your belief in me has meant more than you know.

To everyone at Penguin who helped bring this book to life – Ru Merritt, Liv Nightingall, Emille Bwale and the whole team at Ebury – thank you for believing in me and giving me this incredible opportunity. I feel so lucky to have worked with such a fantastic, passionate team.

To the dream team behind the shoot – my brilliant photographer Hannah Hughes, food stylist Amy Stephenson and prop stylist Max Robinson – your hard work, creativity and attention to detail brought these recipes to life so beautifully. I'm beyond grateful.

To my amazing community on social media – none of this would be possible without you. Every comment, message and recipe you've recreated has meant the world. I wrote this book with you in mind and I'll never stop being thankful for your support.

Writing a cookbook with Penguin has always felt like an unreachable dream, so to be sat here now writing this is incredibly surreal. I've poured my heart into this book, and I hope you can feel that on every page.

This book is about sharing my love of food, without sacrificing what matters most – your time, your family and your friends. Thank you so much for buying this book. I'm forever grateful.

With love,

Hollie x

About the author

Hollie Wood (@dinner_at_hols) is a home cook and mum of two from Rugby with a passion for making dinnertime easier for busy families. With over 15 years of experience creating simple, comforting meals, Hollie has built a loyal following by sharing quick, no-fuss recipes that are full of flavour and ready in no time, online.

EBURY PRESS

UK | USA | Canada | Ireland | Australia
India | New Zealand | South Africa

Ebury Press is part of the Penguin Random House group of companies whose addresses can be found at global.penguinrandomhouse.com

Penguin Random House UK
One Embassy Gardens, 8 Viaduct Gardens, London SW11 7BW

penguin.co.uk

First published by Ebury Press in 2026

1

Copyright © Hollie Wood 2026
Photography © Hannah Rose Hughes 2026

The moral right of the author has been asserted.

Penguin Random House values and supports copyright. Copyright fuels creativity, encourages diverse voices, promotes freedom of expression and supports a vibrant culture. Thank you for purchasing an authorised edition of this book and for respecting intellectual property laws by not reproducing, scanning or distributing any part of it by any means without permission. You are supporting authors and enabling Penguin Random House to continue to publish books for everyone. No part of this book may be used or reproduced in any manner for the purpose of training artificial intelligence technologies or systems. In accordance with Article 4(3) of the DSM Directive 2019/790, Penguin Random House expressly reserves this work from the text and data mining exception.

Editorial Director: Ru Merritt
Senior Editor: Liv Nightingall
Editorial Assistant: Emille Bwale
Production: Lucy Harrison
Design: Double Slice (Amelia Leuzzi and Bonnie Eichelberger)
Photographer: Hannah Rose Hughes
Food Stylist: Amy Stephenson
Prop Stylist: Max Robinson

Colour origination by Altaimage Ltd
Printed and bound in Estonia by Print Best OÜ

The authorised representative in the EEA is Penguin Random House Ireland, Morrison Chambers, 32 Nassau Street, Dublin D02 YH68.

A CIP catalogue record for this book is available from the British Library

ISBN 9781529975734

Penguin Random House is committed to a sustainable future for our business, our readers and our planet. This book is made from Forest Stewardship Council® certified paper.